Copyright Notice	
Potted History	
Getting Ready	
The Maps	6
The Walks	7
Walk 1 – Around the Cathedral (1.5 km)	9
Walk 2 – Under the River (3.3 km or 2.3 km)	60
Walk 3 – The Castle and St Pauls (1.6 km)	87
Walk 4 – Newer Antwerp and Rubens (2.8 km)	112
Too far to Stroll to	170
Did you enjoy these walks?	177
Other Strolling Around Books to try:	178

Copyright Notice

Strolling Around Antwerp by Irene Reid

ISBN: 9798676740993

All rights reserved. This book may not be reproduced in any form, in whole or in part, without written permission from the author.

The author has made every effort to ensure the accuracy of the information in this book at the time of going to press, and cannot accept responsibility for any consequences arising from the use of the book.

Book Cover

Photo by Irene Reid

Enhanced by Prisma Photo Editor

Potted History

Antwerp has been inhabited since Roman times – we know this because archaeologists have unearthed bits of pottery and glass from the second century AD. However it wasn't until the fourth century that someone gave the place a name - at least one that we know about. There are various theories on the meaning of "Antwerp" which you can read about later.

By the end of the Dark Ages Antwerp had become a small village, but it was burned down by the marauding Vikings who pillaged along the coast of Northern Europe. The village was rebuilt, and this time a protective ditch and wall were added for defence.

The Holy Roman Empire was a huge conglomeration of mostly Germanic fiefdoms and countries. The Empire expanded and shrunk over the centuries. In the tenth century it took over part of the Low Countries, including Antwerp. Antwerp survived as a fortification on the border between the Holy Roman Empire and Flanders, defined by the river Scheldt. To help defend the little town, a wooden fortress was erected and later replaced with a stone castle. Later a ditch was dug around the town and a wall erected behind the ditch for additional safety.

By the fourteenth century the little town had grown into one of the most important trading centres in Western Europe. It also became part of wealthy Flanders around about the same time. Bruges, which lay further down the coast, was the commercial hub of Flanders so Antwerp was therefore relegated to second place. However Bruges's luck ran out when its access to the sea silted up leaving it stranded. Antwerp stepped up to take its place; and the merchants and well-off moved to where the money was.

In the fifteenth century, diamond cutting and polishing became one of the city's main businesses. This was down to an invention by Lodewijk van Berken from Bruges which made the process of cutting and polishing diamonds much more reliable. Orders from European nobility for beautiful gemstones flooded into Antwerp, and even today Antwerp has a famous Diamond District where gems are processed.

Life got more difficult in the sixteenth century when the Protestants and the Catholics of Europe fought each other endlessly. The Spanish and their dreaded Inquisition arrived in Flanders, and brought misery and death to anyone who was not a good Catholic. Antwerp was in fact wrecked by the Spanish during this period, and many of Antwerp's richest and brightest upped sticks and headed further north to the safety of Amsterdam.

Antwerp soldiered on under the Spanish, although it didn't regain its position as a major market, because the vital river Scheldt was blockaded by the Dutch cutting off Antwerp's access to the sea.

Napoleon arrived in 1795 with the French army. He modernised Antwerp and reopened the Scheldt by force, but he also pinched many of the city's greatest treasures and shipped them back to Paris.

Flanders was united with the Netherlands in 1815 for a brief period. However Belgium came into being in 1830 and included Antwerp. The Scheldt was closed again by the Dutch in retaliation, and it stayed closed until 1863.

Today, Antwerp is Europe's second largest port after Rotterdam.

Getting Ready

Antwerp Card

It's worth popping into the Tourist office to buy the Antwerp Card if you plan to visit the museums on these walks. You can buy it at the Tourist Office in the Grote Markt, or online at:

https://www.visitantwerpcity.com/antwerp-city-card.html

Ruien

You can venture down into the old Antwerp sewers for a guided tour – don't worry they are no longer in use. However the tour takes a few hours, so make sure you have enough time to see Antwerp above ground as well.

If you are interested, go to the office in Suikerrui to reserve a place, or have a look online at:

http://ruien.be/en/

Wolsack and the Hofkamer

There is a hidden eighteenth century house which you will pass by on walk 1 and which you might want to visit. However visiting hours are very limited and you must pre-book a ticket.

If you are interested here is the link:

https://experienceantwerp.be/en/offers/activities/architecture/the-hofkamer/visit-to-the-hofkamer-individuals/

Paleis op de Meir

This palace is included in Walk 4. You can join a tour but at the time of writing only on Mondays at 10am or 2pm.

Here is the link if you want to book a slot.

https://www.openmonumenten.be/monumenten/paleis-op-de-meir

The Lace Museum

If you plan to visit the Lace Museum in the Carolus Borromeus Church, note that at the time of writing it is only open to the public on Wednesdays. Check the web site for opening times.

https://topa.be/en/sint-carolus-borromeus/rondleidingen/

The Maps

There are maps sprinkled all through the walks to help you find your way. **Remember**, if you need to check where you are at any point during a walk, always flip backwards to find the map you need.

The Walks

Walk 1 – Around the Cathedral - 1.5km

Walk around the Cathedral, the Grote Markt, then through the old streets of Antwerp, visiting one of Antwerp's best museums.

The walk includes the Wolsack which you may already have booked a timeslot to visit. The Wolsack is usually only open to visitors in the afternoon, so you may have to make your way there at some point during the walk. You will never be more than a ten minute walk away from it.

Walk 2 – Under the River - 3.3 km or 2.3 km

Walk through the old town to see a Guttenberg Bible, then an optional walk under the river, and finish with a walk along the riverside.

Walk 3 – The Castle and St Pauls – 1.6 km

Explore the Castle before walking through the oldest part of the old town. Then visit Saint Pauls church and return to Grote Markt by another stroll through the old town.

Walk 4 – Newer Antwerp and Rubens – 2.8 km

Walk down Antwerp's main shopping street before visiting two more of Antwerp's best museums.

Walk 5 - Eclectic Architecture – 1 km

Explore an outlying district of Antwerp which is famous for its very unusual mansions. There are no famous sites to see, just a pleasant stroll along three streets admiring the homes built there.

Too far to Stroll to

Finally there are some really interesting sights which are not easy to reach on foot, but mentioned here in case you want to visit them.

Walk 1 – Around the Cathedral (1.5 km)

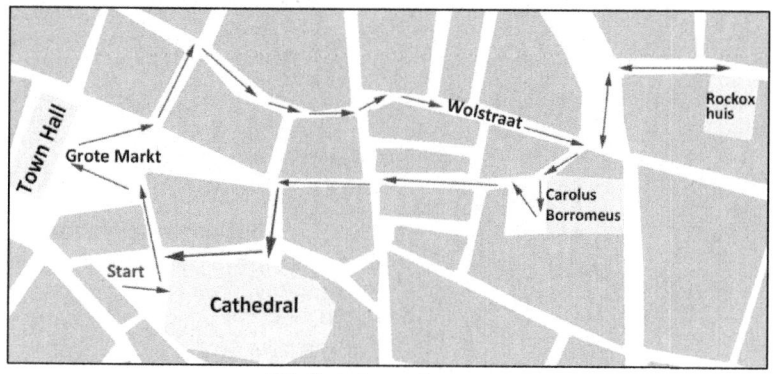

Walk 1 Overview

This walk starts at the Cathedral with its Rubens masterpieces. It then takes you to the main square, the Grote Markt.

From there you make your way east along some of Antwerp's oldest streets, before visiting one of the city's best museums.

You then visit another wonderful old church and finally return to the Cathedral.

[Map 1]

W - Well
S - Statue
D - Doors
P - Plaque

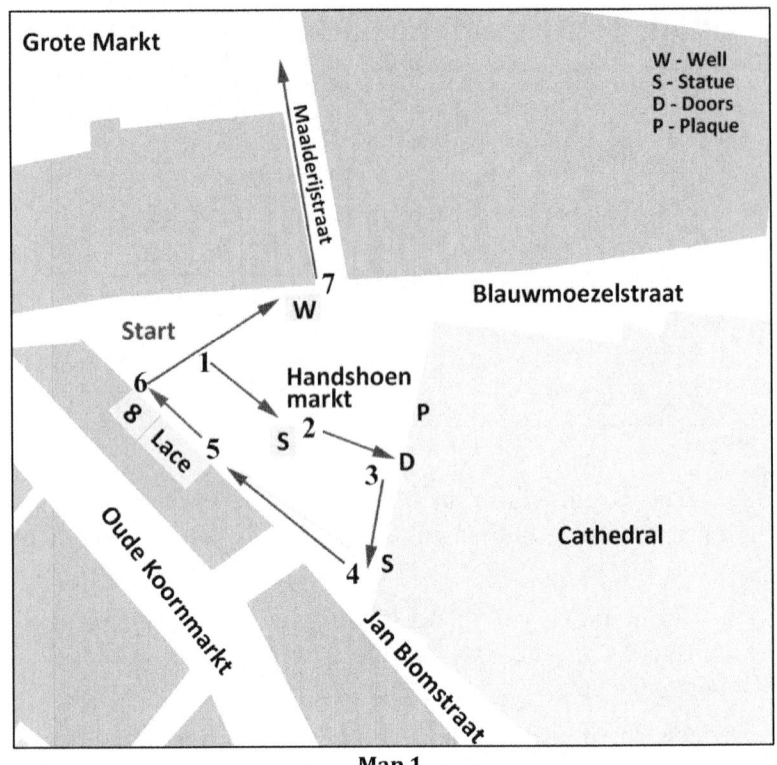

Map 1

Start this walk in the triangular square just in front of the Cathedral.

The square is called Handschoenmarkt which means Glove Market. This is where gloves were sold in the sixteenth century.

Map 1.1 - Walk towards the Cathedral, and as you do you find a rather unusual statue in the middle of the square. It's a little boy and a dog asleep on the cobblestones.

Nello and Patrasche

It's there to commemorate the sad story of Nello (the boy) and Patrasche (his little dog) which is told in the book "A Dog of Flanders".

It is set in Antwerp and was written by a British author named Ouida in the nineteenth century. Although the statue looks very sweet, it's really not a happy story as Ouida wanted to highlight child poverty.

Nello was a poor orphan who adopted a stray starving dog and named him Patrasche. Nello helped his grandfather make a living by selling milk, and Patrasche helped his master by pulling the milk-cart. Nello also loved art and one Christmas Antwerp Cathedral held an exhibition of Rubens's works.

Poor Nello couldn't afford to buy a ticket to see the famous paintings, but on Christmas Eve he found the Cathedral door lying open. Nello and Patrasche sneaked into the icy Cathedral, and next morning their little frozen bodies were found in front of one of the great paintings, "The Descent from the Cross" by Rubens.

Not so long ago there was just a simple plaque here to commemorate that sad story, but the story of Nello and

Patrasche became part of the reading curriculum for Japanese children.

In 1970 it was turned into a Japanese TV series and it became a huge hit. As you might guess, visiting Japanese visitors flocked to take snaps of the plaque. So Antwerp decided to take it a step further and now we have this rather poignant statue.

Map 1.2 - Stand in front of the Cathedral.

Cathedral of Our Lady

The Towering Cathedral stands on the site of the earlier twelfth century Notre Dame chapel. In the fourteenth century it was decided to expand and a new church was planned to match Antwerp's growing status. Two towers were in the original design; however the second tower never made it. Construction was started but the cathedral suffered a catastrophic fire and the second tower burned down before it was completed. It was decided to abandon it altogether.

The church was also ravaged during the protestant revolution of the sixteenth century and many of its treasures were stolen and sold off.

In 1794 the French invaded and plundered the Cathedral yet again. In fact, they even toyed with the idea of demolishing it. However the Cathedral survived and in later years even got some of its treasures back from Paris. It went through a long major restoration project in the last half of the twentieth century, and even now parts of the building are still being cared for.

The Cathedral Exterior

From the outside, the cathedral gets more and more decorative the higher you look. Stand back so you can see the tower properly. It really impressed Charles V, the Holy Roman Emperor. He said that it was so beautiful it should be placed under glass and Napoleon likened it to intricate lace.

The tower holds forty-nine bells. The heaviest is Carolus weighing in at over 7 tons and named after Charles V of France who donated it. It takes a team of 16 bell-ringers to get it moving and ringing out. It's made of a mix of gold, silver and copper and is very valuable. It is only rung on special occasions a few times a year.

Judgement at the Door

Above the main doors is a fascinating vision of the Day of Judgement which is said to lie before us all.

In the centre and on the bottom row sits a monk pointing to a skull – cheerfully reminding us that we are all going to die. On either side of him stands a line of humanity, each person waiting to hear his fate.

Above the monk is the archangel Michael holding the scales by which we will all be judged. Above him sits Jesus deciding everyone's fate. The good people on the left of Michael are very calm and looking forward to a pleasant afterlife, with Saint Peter standing at the side to welcome them in. Those who have a few sins under their belts are on the right-hand side of Michael and the afterlife looks far less appealing with a devil welcoming them to hell.

Running around the scene of judgement day are four arches full of sculptures of the good and the wise. The innermost arch contains the angels, the second has various wise men from the Bible, the third holds the twelve Apostles, and the final arch is full of saints

Between the double doors stands the Virgin Mary. On either side of the doors stand a group of saints who are known as the Antwerp Saints. They get that name because they all lived in Antwerp at some point in their lives. There are two women saints in the group, Saint Walburga and Saint Dymphna.

Dymphna (above) stands on the left-hand side of the door. She was an Irish princess who had to run away from home because her father wanted to commit incest. Her father pursued her to Belgium and eventually cut off her head.

Walburga is on the right-hand side and was an English saint from Devon. Sainthood ran in the family; her Father and Mother were both saints, and even her two brothers were saints!

Go Inside the Cathedral – you will have to buy a ticket unless you have bought an Antwerp Card.

Inside the Cathedral

Inside you will be greeted by lines of white marble pillars which lead you through the church. You can't miss the wonderful pulpit on our right hand side as you walk down the nave.

The Pulpit

The pulpit was actually brought to the cathedral from an abbey which lies to the South of Antwerp.

It is carved from oak, and it has so many figures on it that it is a bit overwhelming at first. It's inspired by nature so we see an oak tree and a beech tree, with the knotty branches and twigs housing a multitude of different birds and little animals – there is even a parrot. It's said that the oak tree and the beech tree were chosen because Saint Bernard once said:

I have no other teachers than the beeches and the oaks

Four female figures hold the pulpit up, one from each of the continents of Europe, Asia, Africa and America, showing that Christianity had spread across the world.

A nice touch is that they are holding hands, to show that Christianity binds them together. Europe holds a sceptre as Europe was seen as the most powerful continent. Asia wears a veil and eastern clothes, America wears a headdress with feathers, and Africa is a native of that continent.

An urban myth has grown over the years that America is a portrayal of Pocahontas, and no one is quite sure how the myth started. It's been said it was an opinion given by a visiting American professor. Another version says it was an American soldier at the end of World War II who claimed she looked like Pocahontas. But officially she is just America.

Right at the top of the pulpit is an angel in a rather peculiar position, almost crashing into the top of the pulpit while blowing a horn.

There are many works of art, but the two you absolutely must see are "The Raising of the Cross" and "The Descent from the Cross" both by Rubens. Continue to walk down the centre of the cathedral to reach them – you will find them on either side of the steps leading to the altar.

Rubens

Peter Paul Rubens was actually born in Germany, as his parents fled there from Antwerp during the religious upheavals of the sixteenth century. His father was a Calvinist, so when Catholic Spain took over Antwerp getting out of the country seemed the wise thing to do.

His father died in Germany, so Rubens and his mother returned to Antwerp where he studied and eventually set up his studio. Ironically Rubens then became a devout catholic.

He travelled to Italy to study the famous masterpieces there. He stayed in Italy for eight years but returned when he heard that his mother was very ill. Sadly she died before he got home.

The Raising of the Cross - Rubens

This triptych was actually painted for the church of Saint Walburga, one of the Antwerp Saints whose statue you saw at the door. That church used to stand in front of Antwerp castle but it was demolished in 1815.

In the central panel you can see the cross bearing Christ being hauled upright. Rubens shows us the executioners straining at the ropes, and holding Christ's body in place as the cross is pulled and pushed slowly upright. Jesus's eyes look up to heaven, on the left the mourners weep and watch, and on the right the Roman officer issues commands to the men raising the cross.

The execution notice is nailed to the top of the cross and reads:

> Jesus of Nazareth, king of the Jews

It was placed there to mock him by order of Pilate. According to the Book of John it was written in Aramaic, Greek, and Latin to make sure everyone could read it. The Latin version is:

> Iesus Nazarenus Rex Iudaeorum

Rubens has depicted the notice flapping in the breeze with the last word of Latin, "Iudeorum", only partially visible. If you were to look at a crucifix in a church today you will see that the entire notice has usually been replaced by the initials INRI - the first letters of the above Latin.

Another interesting detail is the sun and moon on the top left corner of the right hand panel – yes a total eclipse is about to happen. Rubens has included it because it was believed that the darkness which the Bible tells us descended during the crucifixion was caused by an eclipse.

When Napoleon the Magpie arrived, he stripped Antwerp of many of its treasures and carted them off to the Louvre in Paris. It was not until his defeat at Waterloo that they were returned, as were many, many other paintings to cities across Europe.

The Descent from the Cross - Rubens

In "The Descent from the Cross" we see eight grieving people gently lowering Chris's lifeless body to the ground. His skin is deathly white.

The figure in the bright red robe is the disciple John, on the left is the Virgin Mary reaching out to her son, and Mary Magdalen kneels below holding his foot. Rubens followed convention in depicting Mary Magdalen as a blonde despite the distinct unlikeliness of blonde hair in Israel at that time. The woman behind Mary Magdalen has delicate teardrops on her cheeks.

If you look at the right hand bottom corner you will see a plate, and in it are the Crown of Thorns and the nails from the cross. Beside it lies the "Jesus of Nazareth, king of the Jews" notice.

There are two other notable paintings by Rubens for you to find, The Resurrection Triptych, and the Assumption of the Virgin.

From The Descent from the Cross, make your way towards the back of the cathedral. You will find The Resurrection Triptych in the second chapel on your right.

The Resurrection Triptych - Rubens

This painting was commissioned by the very wealthy and important Plantin family – you will read more about them later on another walk. It formed part of the funeral monument of Jan and Martina Plantin.

Rubens shows us Jesus striding from the tomb. He is surrounded by a glowing halo of light to the astonishment and fear of the soldiers guarding the tomb.

Notice the soldier right at the front who is trying to crawl away in fear. Rubens used a very skilful technique to give the impression that the soldier is backing out of the painting towards the viewer.

Continue towards the back of the cathedral to reach a point where you can get a close look at the Assumption of the Virgin which is on the high altar.

The Assumption of the Virgin - Rubens

In the Assumption of the Virgin, a choir of little angels lifts the Virgin Mary towards heaven, while the apostles and other biblical characters gather beneath her to see her off.

Mary Magdalene is there with her beautiful blonde hair. One oddity is the fact that Rubens wife, Isabella Brandt, died while this painting was being created and Rubens painted her face on the woman in the centre wearing a bright red dress.

Make your way to stand as close to the high dome just before the altar as you can.

Another Assumption

It is the highest point of the Cathedral and it is where they chose to put another version of The Assumption. It's very appropriate as Mary soars up to heaven, but it does make it very difficult to see the painting. When Napoleon's looters were grabbing all the art they could lay their hands on to ship back to Paris, they decided to leave that one behind.

Map 1.3 - When you exit the Cathedral, turn left to find a statue of the many workers who built the Cathedral.

The Cathedral Builders

It is dedicated to father and son Jan and Peiter Appelmans, who were the cathedral's architects. Pieter Appelmans stands on a wall giving instructions to his stonemasons.

Map 1.4 - Face away from the Cathedral Builders and walk along the edge of the square to reach a little shop called Kantwinkeltje, Antwerp's Lace Shop.

Flemish Lace

In the sixteenth to eighteenth century Antwerp was one of the main centres of Flemish Lace-making. It's said that at its peak, 50% of the population was involved in some part of lace production. However when the Dutch blockaded the river Scheldt the lace could no longer be shipped overseas and its manufacture collapsed.

Making lace by hand is an incredibly labour-intensive and skilful job and most lace sold today is manufactured and imported from the far east, but you can still find places which make and sell the Flemish version – if you can afford the prices.

Kantwinkeltje

The same family have been making and selling lace from this shop since the nineteenth century. You might want to have a look in the windows to see if something catches your eye.

Map 1.5 - Just next to the lace shop at number 8 is a beer shop called Belgian Beers and Brews.

Belgian Beers and Brews

This little shop has a very good selection of bottled Belgian beers on their shelves. They also sell the glass each beer should be drunk from - they make a great souvenir.

You could pay for a "degustation" which is a tasting of several beers, although it might be wiser to save that treat until you complete your exploring for the day, as Belgian beer is very strong!

Map 1.6 - Stand with the beer shop behind you. Cross the square diagonally right to find an old well.

Matsijs's well

It is topped with some decorative ironwork illustrating a character known as Brabo. Who was Brabo? Of course there is a legend:

A giant called Antigoon extracted a huge toll from ships wishing to reach Antwerp, and if they refused to pay the giant chopped off the sailors' hands.

This was clearly bad for business. Silvius Brabo, who was reputably a nephew of Julius Caesar, fought and defeated Antigoon. He then took revenge for all the mutilated sailors by chopping one of the giant's hands off and tossing it into the river. On the well Brabo is depicted as throwing the giant's hand. You will see a much bigger version of Brabo in action later on this walk.

The well is known as "Matsijs's well" and is part of a romantic story. Matsijs was a founder of the Antwerp School whose most famous member was Rubens.

Matsijs started out as a blacksmith but he fell in love with the daughter of an artist. The artist would not contemplate his daughter marrying a blacksmith even though she loved him. So to win over the artist, Matsijs stopped working iron and became an artist himself. He was very successful and they were happily wed. Many years later Matsijs forged the ironwork now adorning the well to show that he was still a gifted blacksmith as well as a gifted artist.

Matsijs died in 1529. In 1629, one hundred years later, his life was celebrated with a ceremony and a plaque on the facade of the Antwerp Cathedral. It's just to the left of the main doorway and it reads:

> Connubialis amor de Mulcibre fecit Apellem

Mulcibre is another name for Vulcan, the god of fire. Apelles was a famous painter from ancient Greece who painted Alexander the Great. So it has been very loosely translated as

> Love made a painter of the blacksmith

Beneath his image you can see the tools of both his trades; on the left his palette and on the right his blacksmith tools. An asteroid was named after him: asteroid 9569 Quintenmatsijs.

Map 1.7 - Standing beside the well you will see two streets leading away from the square, Blauwmoezelstraat which runs down one side of the Cathedral, and Maalderijstraat which runs away from the cathedral.

Walk along Maalderijstraat and you will enter the large square called Grote Markt.

Map 2

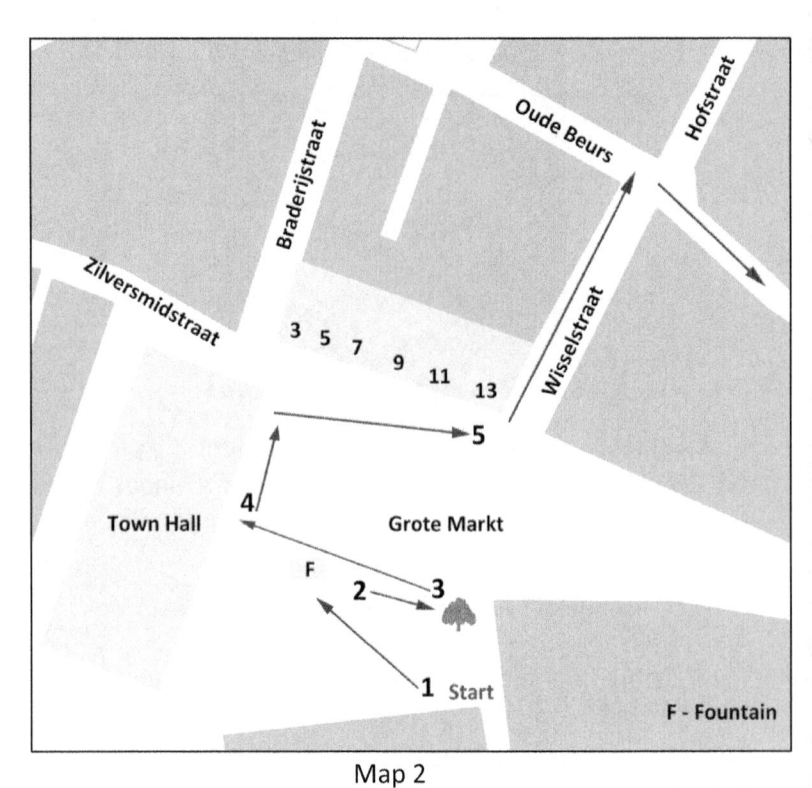

Map 2.1 - Walk over to the fountain which is topped with a bronze statue and which stands in front of the Town Hall.

Brabo

Here is Brabo in action once more. The statue was created by Jef Lambeaux, the same sculptor who created The Cathedral Builders.

In 1585 the Dutch imposed a toll on any ship trying to use the River Scheldt to reach Antwerp - which had a catastrophic effect on Antwerp's trade. The Dutch did not lift that toll until 1863, and a few years later Antwerp commissioned this fountain to celebrate the liberation of the river.

The fountain Brabo stands on is unusual in that there is no water catchment basin; the water just drains away under the stones.

Brabo stands on top of a pedestal with marine animals and the dying giant at the bottom. Antigoon is grasping his arm from which his hand has been chopped off. Above him, mermaids are holding up a castle which represents Antwerp, and above the castle stands Brabo getting ready to hurl the giant's hand into the water, symbolising the freedom of the river.

The hand was incorporated into the city seal, and the city confectioners started making Antwerpse Handjes, little chocolate hands which you can buy in the city's chocolate shops.

The legend of Brabo is also one explanation on how Antwerp got its name, Antwerp literally means Hand Throw. However the less romantic thinkers believe it comes from the Latin word antverpia, which describes a piece of land on the inside curve of a river. The Scheldt riverbed previously followed a different path and it would have put Antwerp on a curve of the river. So perhaps they are right.

Map 2.2 - *Stand in front of Brabo and face away from the Town hall. In front of you stands the Liberation Tree.*

Liberation Tree

The tree commemorates the 50th Anniversary of liberation after World War II. There is a plaque beneath it which reads:

Liberation Tree
50th Anniversary of the liberation of Antwerp
September 3, 1994

After the Normandy landings the Allies recaptured France and Belgium at an astonishing rate, and Allied supply lines became precarious. It was vital to gain control of a large port to allow supplies to be shipped in, and Antwerp fitted the bill.

General Montgomery ordered the Allies to retake Antwerp, and with the help of the Belgian resistance the German Army was defeated and the city was freed. The people of Antwerp came into the streets waving the Belgian flag to greet the liberators. They showered flowers onto the incoming tanks and the delighted soldiers received many kisses to celebrate the liberation.

However the German army still held control of the river banks, both in Antwerp and further up-river. This meant they could block any ships trying to enter or leave Antwerp. It took until November to finally dislodge them and open the river to shipping once more. The liberation of Antwerp and its river was a vital part of the Allied push towards Germany.

Map 2.3 - Now turn your attention to the Town Hall which fills the side of the Grote Markt behind Brabo.

Town Hall

Antwerp became the leading financial centre in the Low Countries in the fifteenth century when nearby Bruges went into decline.

The first Town Hall was deemed far too small for such an important city, so the city fathers decided that a new one was required and plans were made. However, the plans had to be put on hold as war erupted in the sixteenth century - the Spanish invaded. The building materials bought for the new Town Hall were diverted to the war effort for the city's defence.

Finally the Spanish won the war, and once peace settled the Town Hall plans were revamped and a Renaissance building was constructed in 1565. However, its first incarnation was very short-lived as it was gutted by the Spaniards just eleven years later in "The Spanish Fury".

Catholic Spain may have ruled over this part of Flanders but Spain was in deep financial trouble. They were not helped by protestant England's navy intercepting Spanish ships, sacking, and sinking them. The Spanish navy ran out of money, so the sailors decided to sack various Flemish cities as recompense – including Antwerp. The way in which this was done was so destructive that it is called "The Spanish Fury".

There were two important consequences. Firstly the Flemish people in occupied Flanders grew to loathe the Spanish Monarchy and rebelled. Secondly Antwerp was so devastated by the destruction that Amsterdam, safely further north, was able to step in as the principle market and business centre in the Low Countries.

However, at the end of all this bloodshed, in 1579 Antwerp did finally rebuild its town hall and you see the result today. It required lots of finance, so a deal was struck

- the ground floor was built to house little shops. You can see the line of little doors running along the front of the building. The city finances gained rent from the shopkeepers, and the shopkeepers gained a prime retail location. The shops are all gone now.

Stand in front and look up, you can see three female figures above you, Justice, Prudence, and centre-stage is the Virgin Mary.

Originally the central position was taken by another statue of Brabo, but he was ousted and replaced by the Virgin Mary in 1587 when the Catholic Church gained the upper hand.

Justice and Prudence

Justice and Prudence are there as they are seen as excellent qualities for councillors. Justice carries her sword and scales and their meaning is pretty self-explanatory. Prudence on the other hand is holding a mirror and a snake which is less obvious. The snake usually gets a bad press but in this context it represents wisdom. The mirror represents the ability to look to the past for guidance and to look ahead to see the consequences of any actions.

The facade is usually brightly decorated with the flags of countries in the EU, and those who have a consulate in Antwerp. The Town hall originally had a courtyard but it was covered over in the nineteenth century. It is not open to the public but the reception rooms can be used for weddings and receptions, so you might see a bride or two when you are in the square.

Map 2.4 - Face away from the Town Hall and turn left to find the most interesting block of guild-houses with their sparkling statues at the top.

Guild Houses

As in most Belgian Towns the guilds built their guild houses around the main square, and Antwerp is no different. Those you see all around the square are relatively new, as most of the originals were destroyed in the Spanish Fury.

Witten Engel (3)

The first building which sits on the left hand corner was called the Witten Engel (White Angel). The golden angel at the top reflects that name - she seems to be reading from a banner she is holding in her hands.

Cuypershuys (5)

Next door was the guild-house of the Coopers. At the top is a statue of Saint Matthias who was chosen as the replacement apostle by the remaining eleven apostles after Judas's treachery. He is the Coopers' patron saint.

The Crossbowmen (7)

Number 7 is the tallest guild house on the square.

It was the house of the Crossbowmen and near the top you can see two armed crossbowmen. Right at the top is a bronze statue of Saint George and the dragon - it was also made by Jef Lambeaux who sculpted the Brabo statue, and it weighs in at a whacking 1000 kilos!

De Spiegel (9)

Number 9 next door is called De Spiegel, The Mirror, and this was the guild-house of the longbow men. Their patron saint is Saint Sebastian who was sentenced to death by Emperor Diocletian. Sebastian was tied to a tree, shot by arrows, and left to die. You can see a gilded Saint Sebastian pierced by arrows at the top of the guild house.

Den Arend (11)

The Meerseniers guild-house at number 11 has five golden statues – a Meersenier was a local tradesman. This is one of the few buildings on the square which survived the Spanish Fury. Centuries later it was sold to Eugene Kreglinger who demolished it and had a new building erected in its place, but he did recreate the original façade. The statues at the top are four craftsmen of the guild, blacksmith, painter, shipper, farmer, and topped by an eagle.

Huis de Vos (13)

The House of the Fox is next door at number 13. It only got that name in the nineteenth century when an inn called The Fox moved in and the gilded fox was put on the gable. Previously it was the guild house of the halberdiers – they were soldiers who used a long type of spear in battle.

This is currently the tourist office, so you might want to pop in if you haven't already.

Map 2.5 – Stand in the Grote Markt and face the Huis de Vos. Walk down Wisselstraat on its right-hand side to reach a crossroads. Turn right into Oude Beurs.

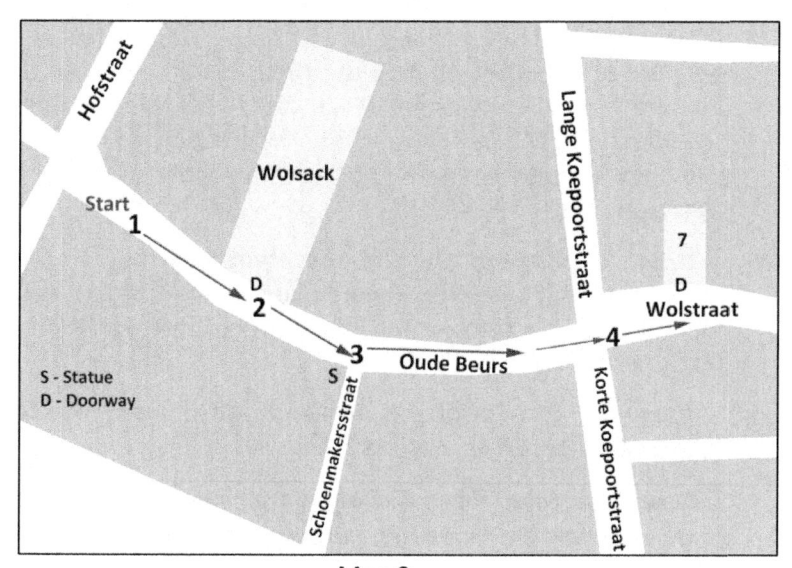

Map 3

Map 3.1 - At number 27 on your left you will find an old ornate gateway which is the entrance to the Wolsack.

Wolsack

Antwerp's wool trade with England was centred along this street and Wolstraat which lies a little further along.

Behind this door was an old warehouse complex where they stored the wool - notice the ram's head at the top of the door. In 1772 François Adrien van den Bogaert, a very rich merchant, decided to renovate the complex and turn it into both a family home and a reception hall, all set in a pretty garden.

It is possible to visit the reception hall, but at the moment its only open during the summer months and you must have pre-booked a time slot – details are in the Get Ready section.

If you do not wish to visit or plan to do so later, skip to "Along Oude Beurs" on page 38.

Otherwise enter the gateway to walk through the little garden towards the Hofkamer, Bogaert's reception hall.

The Hofkamer

Bogaert built it to impress his business clients. Stand in the garden at the front of the house and look up – it has so many windows and glass was so expensive!

On the balcony above the door you will see two figures, the Savage and the Wild Woman. If you were to look at Antwerp's coat of arms you would see these two characters holding Antwerp's shield. The two figures you see are copies of the originals which are now safely in a museum.

The clock above the door is interesting - it is topped by an armillary sphere which is a representation of the universe and the orbits of the planets. It is supposed to represent Antwerp as a world power.

Inside was once a treasure trove of rich frescoes and marble, but sadly a lot has been lost. The ceiling of one of the rooms held the largest single canvas painting in Belgium. It is 65 square meters in size and it portrays "The Gods of Mount Olympus". It was carefully restored recently and has now been rehung in the Hofkamer, so make your way inside to find it.

You can gaze up to see the many Greek Gods and Goddesses in glorious Trompe-l'œil effect. In the centre is Zeus surrounded by his fellow gods and goddesses.

37

No-one knows who actually painted it. The restorers have revealed some parts of the gods which had been "hidden" for centuries for modesty's sake. The room which houses "The Gods" also hosts a beautiful fireplace in gorgeous white Carrera marble. It's topped with a huge gilded mirror.

One curiosity of the Hofkamer which is not to be missed is the Boekentoilet – which certainly shows a sense of humour! The walls are lined with fake bookshelves and the loo is hidden beneath a stack of books. It's just above the staircase, so make sure you have a look.

Along Oude Beurs

Map 3.2 - With the door of the Wolsack behind you turn left to continue along Oude Beurs. Pause when you reach number 48 which sits at the corner of Schoenmakersstraat on your right.

As you wander round the streets of the old town you will probably notice that there is a statue of the Virgin Mary on many street corners like this one. Her presence is not because Antwerpens were excessively religious but because of a tax dodge. It seems street lights were taxed by the council, but religious shrines were exempt. So whenever someone decided they wanted a street light outside their home, they also put up a statue attached to the light to dodge the tax!

Map 3.3 - Continue to the next crossroads and cross over into Wolstraat. The trams run along this narrow street so take care.

Wolstraat used to be full of warehouses and was where the English wool merchants stored and traded their product.

Map 3.4 - Continue along to number 7 on your left.

Wolstraat 7

This street has several impressive stone doorways and the first one is on this building which is called "den Tennen Pot". It is a baroque stone doorway from the seventeenth century which is decorated with two lion heads. It is currently a bookstore.

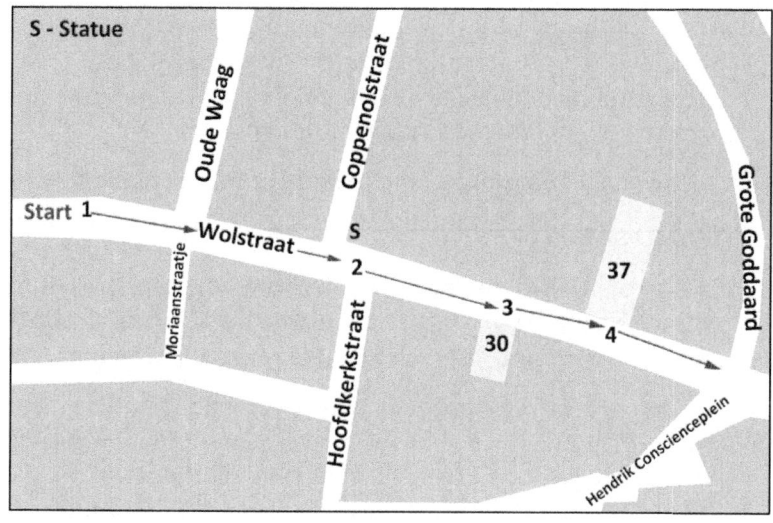

Map 4

Map 4.1 - Continue along Wolstraat passing Oude Waag on your left. The next street on your left is called Coppenolstraat.

Virgin Mary Shrine

On the corner is a shrine to the Virgin Mary with a non-taxable street light. It's a particularly pretty shrine with both Mary and Jesus wearing crowns and sheltering under a blue canopy with a sunburst above it. Baby Jesus is holding some roses which he is giving to his mother.

Map 4.2 - Keep walking along Wolstraat passing Hoofdkerkstraat on your right. Pause at number 30 on your right

Wolstraat 30

This building was once called the "Scilt van Londen" and is where the English wool merchants did a lot of business. It has a beautiful stone door and just like the door at number 7 it is decorated with two lion heads. The decoration also includes angels holding grapes which refer back to an inn which was once located here.

Map 4.3 - Continue along to number 37 on your left.

Wolstraat 37

The old door which has Bontwerkers written above it is nothing special, but push it open and walk down the little passageway to find yourself in a lovely secret garden.

The whole complex belonged to the Furriers (fur workers) guild. The houses which surround the garden were built for poor or sick members of the guild in the fifteenth century. In the middle of the garden is a pump for fresh water.

Map 4.4 - Return to Wolstraat and continue to the next crossroads with Grote Goddaard and Hendrik Conscienceplein.

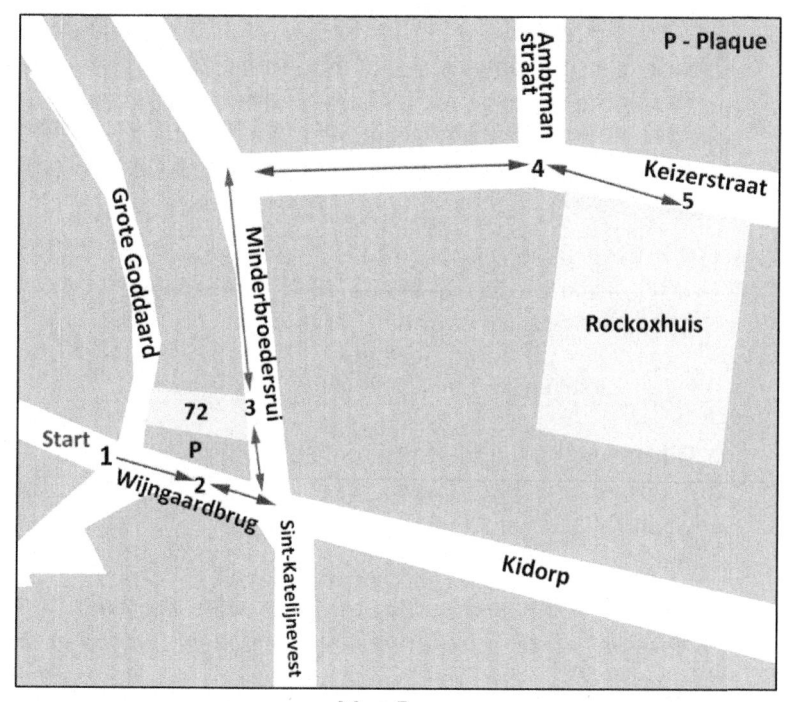

Map 5

Map 5.1 – Carefully cross over into tiny Wijngaardbrug - it means Vineyard Bridge.

If you were to venture onto the Sewer Tour mentioned in the Get Ready section, you would walk under this street. Your guide will point out the remains of the original bridge, one of several which gave access over the canal which surrounded old Antwerp.

For now though look to the left-hand wall and you will find a plaque.

Albrecht Durer Plaque

Dürer was one of the most famous artists in Europe in the sixteenth century, and he spent a year in Antwerp in 1520.

He actually stayed at Wolstraat 19 which you have already passed, however that house has long gone and there is nothing to mark his stay there. This plaque was given to Antwerp by Dürer's home town, Nürnberg, in 1971 to commemorate his visit. It is in Dutch and German and translates as:

> Albrecht Dürer 1471-1528 painter
> lived in Antwerp from 1520-1521 with Joost Planckfelt (Blanckwalt) businessman and soap boiler
> in the house "Engelenborgh" now Wolstraat 19

Dürer kept a detailed diary of his year-long stay and it records his acquaintance with Quinten Matsijs, the blacksmith who became an artist and who you read about earlier.

Map 5.2 - The next part of this walk will take you to the Rockoxhuis, which is an interesting art gallery located in an old house. If you are not keen on art you can skip this section by jumping to "To Hendrick Conscienceplein" on page 50.

Otherwise to visit the museum, continue along a few steps to reach the end of Wijngaardbrug and then turn left into Minderbroedersrui.

Don't miss the handsome restored house on the left hand side at number 72 as you turn into Minderbroedersrui.

Cleyn Clocke

It has beautiful stone balconies, a wooden door, and windows with stained glass. The name of the house is in golden letters just above the ground floor windows.

Map 5.3 - Continue along Minderbroedersrui and then turn into Keizerstraat which is the first street on your right.

Map 5.4 Pass Ambtmanstraat on your left. The Rockoxhuis Museum is a few steps further on the right hand side of Keizerstraat.

Rockoxhuis

This lovely museum was the home of Rockox, one of Antwerp's mayors in the sixteenth century. He was a respected art collector and knew all the major artists of the day. He gathered his own personal collection which is housed in this museum. He was also responsible for commissioning some of the best artwork on public display in Antwerp – including Rubens' "Descent from the Cross" which you saw in the cathedral.

If you go in you will be given a very good guidebook to help you explore the rooms. Here are some favourites worth looking for:

Proverbs – Breughel

Proverbs were very, very popular in Breughel's time and so far about 112 have been identified in this painting. Spot the following which we know in English as:

- To put a spoke in someone's wheel; lower right
- Banging one's head against a brick wall; lower left
- Armed to the teeth; lower left

Right in the middle of the painting you see a man being dressed in a blue cloak by his wife – that apparently means she is not being faithful.

Antwerp harbour – Hans Bol

The river Scheldt is full of ships and in the foreground we see fishermen busy at work.

Sadly most of the towers you see in this depiction of Antwerp's waterfront have now gone. If you visit the other side of the Scheldt on another of the walks, you can see that those that survived.

Christ on the Cross – Rubens

Mary Magdalene is shown kissing Christ's feet.

As you will see later in another more famous painting in the cathedral, Rubens always painted Mary Magdalene with beautiful blonde hair. The Virgin Mary is weeping at the side in her traditional blue robe.

Distribution of Loaves to the Poor – David Vinckboons

Compare this painting to Breughel's busy Proverbs. It has been said that Vinckboons tried to emulate Breughel's storytelling, by showing a crowd of people all busy with their own little stories and interests.

The Education of Jupiter - Jacob Jordaens

Even the Gods have problems with their parents.

The god Saturn ate his children as soon as they were born because he had been told by Earth, his mother, that one of them would become more powerful than he was.

Legend tells us that Jupiter was saved because his mother replaced him with a stone wrapped in blankets, which Saturn happily crunched.

Jupiter was sent to safety in Crete where he was raised by nymphs. Here we see him being educated on Crete. The goat in the background helpfully suckled Jupiter while he was there.

The Meir in Antwerp – Erasmus De Bie

You will visit Meir, Antwerp's busy shopping street, if you tackle walk 4.

This is a vision of Meir of long ago, so try to remember what it used to look like when you get there.

Two studies of a man's head - Anthony Van Dyck

This is simply such an accomplished painting – compare it to portraits by today's artists.

Artists often practised key parts of a large painting. This was a sort of warm-up exercise as Van Dyck prepared to paint a much larger work which would include the same man's head.

The Holy Virgin with the Child Jesus - Quinten Matsijs

This golden painting on a plate is so pretty! You saw Matsijs's Well at the start of this walk and know his story. This is an example of how good an artist he was.

The Garden and the Owl

The museum also has a little courtyard and garden. If you go there, try to find the gorgeous little owl painted on the outside of a window looking in, and his reflection looking back.

Map 5.5 - When you leave the museum turn left along Keizerstraat to return to Minderbroedersrui. Turn left and walk down Minderbroedersrui.

When you reach the crossroads once more, turn right into the little street called Wijngaardbrug where you saw the Durer plaque earlier.

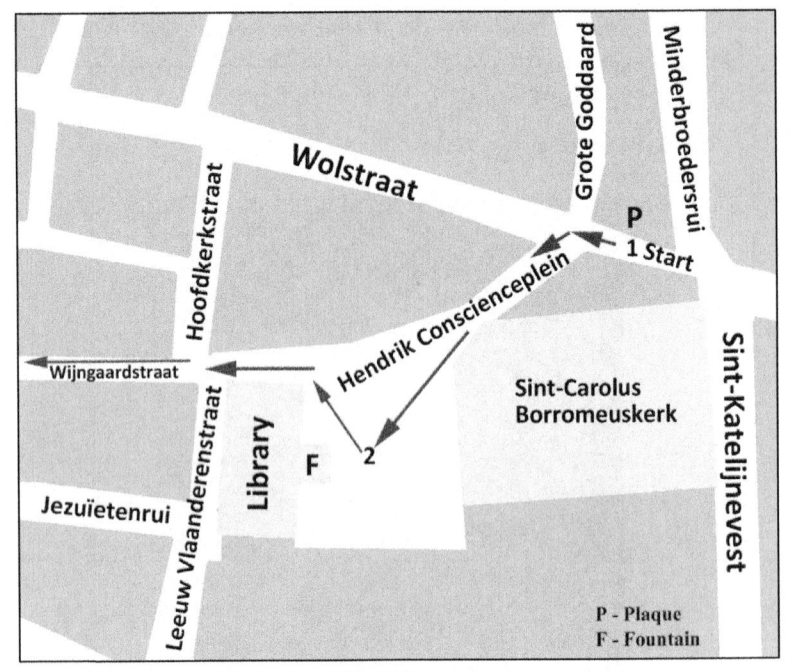

Map 6

To Hendrick Conscienceplein

Map 6.1 - With the Durer plaque on your right-hand side, walk to the crossroads just a few steps in front of you. Turn left to walk into Hendrik Conscienceplein and you will reach a pleasant square.

This square used to be a market square. It was pedestrianised in the sixties because the locals protested over the growing noise of the cars. It's now one of the nicest squares in the city.

Hendrik Conscience

It's named after the much loved Flemish writer Hendrik Conscience, who fought to keep Flemish alive at a time when French was overwhelming the country. In fact at one point Flemish was banned.

The book which captured Flemish hearts was "The Lion of Flanders", which tells the history of the Battle of the Golden Spurs, when the Flemish people stood up to the mighty French army and won! The book made the Flemish people realise that they were a nation

The city library is directly in front of you as you enter the square – it has Stadsbiblioteek inscribed above the door. In front of it sits a statue of Hendrik Conscience with a book in his hand. The statue was erected before Hendrik died but sadly he was too ill to see it. He is buried in Schoonselhof which lies in the south of the city.

Nottebohm

Inside the library there is a wonderful reading room called the Nottebohm. As you will learn later Antwerp was a major centre of book publishing long ago, so it's fitting that it should have such a beautiful place to read the books. Unfortunately at the time of writing, you cannot visit it unless you are part of a pre-arranged group tour.

Opposite the library is the Carolus Borromeus Church.

Carolus Borromeus Church

Antwerp was invaded by Spain in 1584 and the townspeople were given a choice, convert to Catholicism or leave the city. Given that ultimatum about half the population fled the city.

The Jesuits saw their chance and stepped in to build the Ignatius church - Ignatius was the founder of the Jesuits. Their intent was to impress the locals on the strength of the Catholic Church.

The Jesuits' often employed a little trickery in their church construction to emphasize its grandeur, and this church is no different. Standing at the front it looks very imposing, but that is partly due to the top pediment which raises its height. If you were to walk around the church you would see that the pediment is just a frontage with nothing behind it – like a film set.

The façade is also covered in scallops, fruit, horns of plenty, saints and angels. There are even golden cauldrons, a candelabrum, and a pineapple.

The angel on the right is holding the three nails used in the crucifixion and the one on the left holds the lance which was used to wound Christ. Saint Peter and Saint Paul are on either side of the door. Of course Saint Peter is the one holding the keys to the gates of heaven.

Right in the middle is the Jesuit shield, adorned with the golden letters IHS – the first three letters of the name Jesus in Greek.

Go inside.

Inside Carolus Borromeus Church

A lot of the interior was designed by Rubens. Have a look at the enormous pulpit which is one of Rubens' designs. He also painted two of the four altarpieces which were installed in a clever mechanism behind the altar. It allowed the clergy to switch between the four paintings, depending on the sermon being preached – a kind of early PowerPoint presentation.

Rubens' studio and students adorned the church ceiling with 39 paintings – one of the students was Van Dyck.

The church caught fire in 1718 thanks to a bolt of lightning. Sadly the interior was severely damaged and the 39 ceiling paintings were lost, but the altarpieces were saved. The church was repaired but it never regained its former glory – they used stone rather than marble! The Jesuits later sold it and it was renamed the Carolus Borromeus Church.

The Rubens altarpieces were also sold and are now in the Kunsthistorisches Museum in Vienna. At the moment there are just three paintings in the altarpiece mechanism.

There are a lot of confessionals! They are guarded by angels who do their best to make you confess your sins using hints on the alternative. Spot the angel looking at a skull and worms – a warning? Another has a shovel and a pile of bones. Then there is the angel wiping the slate clean - confess and all will be forgiven!

The church burned again in 2009 - but nothing of major importance was lost that time.

If you are here on a Sunday, catch the Artists' mass on at 11:30. There are also often concerts so check inside for details.

Our Lady's Chapel

Don't miss Our Lady's Chapel which is on the right-hand side as you walk down the nave. Fortunately the fire of 1718 missed this beautiful chapel,

It's full of marble carvings, flowers, angels, grapes and colour and you could easily spend some time just gazing at the little figures and decorations. Perhaps the church was originally all this colourful.

The chapel holds a copy of The Assumption of Mary by Rubens. The Assumption is the dramatic moment when the Virgin Mary passes away and is taken up into heaven.

The original was bought by Empress Mary Theresa and it now hangs in the Hermitage Museum in Saint Petersburg.

At the start of the twentieth century the church parishioners paid to have the original painting copied and placed here.

Lace Museum

If you are really keen on lace you should visit the crypt which is where the lace museum is housed. Two lace experts, Nora and Godelieve, will show you around and explain the techniques and complexity of the whole process.

Note, at the time of writing the lace museum is only open on Wednesdays.

Feeling a bit tired now? Sit outside on the benches near Hendrik and enjoy the ambience of the square. Sometimes there is a jazz concert on.

Map 6.2 - When you want to move on, stand with the church door behind you. Cross the square diagonally right to go down the side of the library. Pass Leeuw van Vlaanderenstraat on your right and walk into Wijngaardstraat.

Map 7

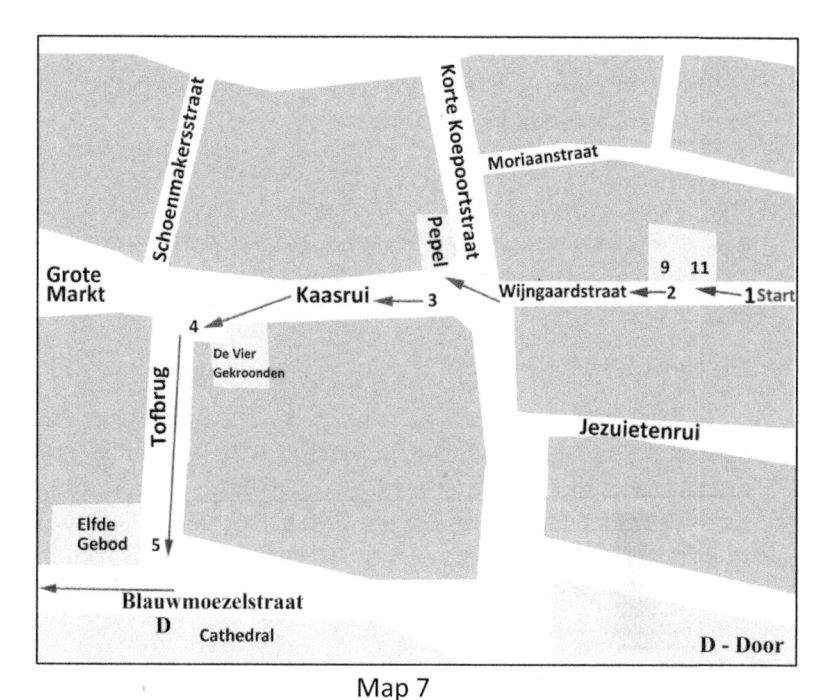

Map 7.1 - Pause at number 11 on your right.

Wijngaardstraat 11

This little jewellers shop is of interest if you like Art Nouveau architecture. It has a beautiful wooden façade in curving Nouveau style.

Wijngaardstraat 9

Next door is another beautiful art nouveau building. Look up to see the striking ironwork decoration.

It was once a tobacco warehouse which was built for two brothers who were tobacco merchants, Stanislas and Hippplyte Pauwels.

The family business was begun by their grandfather Marcus, so they had a stone engraving of his name, M. Pauwels, placed above the door.

Map 7.2 - Continue along Wijngaardstraat to reach a crossroads with Korte Koepoortstraat where once again you will see tramlines. Cross over Korte Koepoortstraat into Kaasrui and take a look the first building on the right hand corner.

De Pepel – The Pepper

It was built in 1860 for the Schoesetters brothers. The Schoesetters were a printing family who specialised in books for schools and the church. They started their business on this site in 1766. When they commissioned their new premises they had it decorated with reliefs celebrating the printing trade – look up to the first floor to see them.

Map 7.3 - Continue along Kaasrui. It will widen out just before Tofbrug. On your left you will see a very narrow oddly shaped building in the corner; it is called De Vier Gekroonden.

De Vier Gekroonden – The Four Crowned

This was the guild-house of the Master Builders who were stonemasons and architects such as Jan Applemans who was involved in building the Cathedral.

The guild-house took its name from "The Four Crowned" who were four Christian stonemasons who refused to carve a statue of the God Aesculapius. So they were tortured to death by order of Emperor Diocletian who never missed an opportunity to create a Christian martyr or two. They became the patron saints of both stonemasons and sculptors.

Map 7.4 – Walk down Torfbrug to find the Elfde Gebod pub. It's at the end of the street on your right-hand side.

Elfde Gebod

It's said to be the oldest pub in Antwerp, and the building it is in has been standing there since 1425. The pub name translates as the 11th commandment, which is said to have been given to Antwerp and states:

> Thou shalt drink beer and enjoy thy life

You will find it is crammed with all sorts of biblical statues and paintings. You might want to return in the evening and sip a beer sitting beside the Virgin Mary.

Map 7.5 – Stand with the pub on your right and you will see one of the Cathedral's orante doors in front of you.

Turn right along Blauwmoezelstraat to return to the front of the cathedral on Handschoenmarkt.

You have now reached the end of this walk.

Walk 2 –Under the River (3.3 km or 2.3 km)

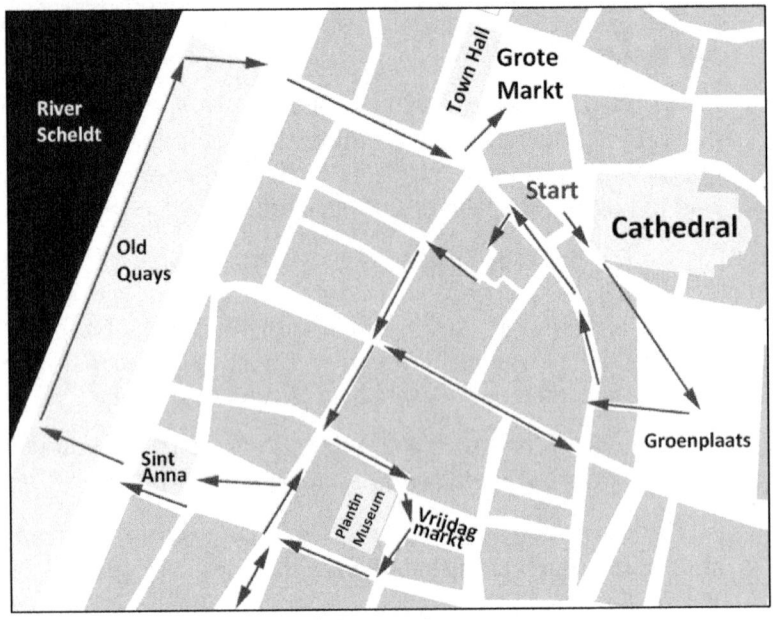

Walk 2 Overview

This walk takes you through more old streets to the wonderful Plantin-Moretus Museum and then down to the river where you can venture to the other side of Antwerp by a tunnel and back again.

You then walk along the elevated river walkway before returning to the Grote Markt.

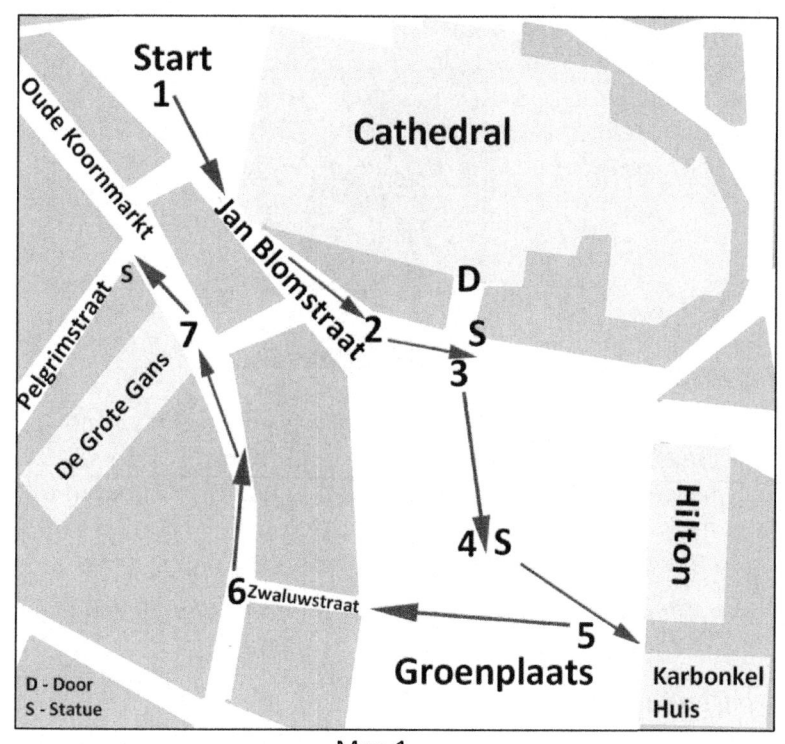

Map 1

The walk starts at the front of the Cathedral.

Map 1.1 - Stand facing the Cathedral door and turn right to walk around the Cathedral on Jan Blomstraat.

Pass little Papenstraatje on your right and you will walk into a large square called Groenplaats.

Map 1.2 - Keep to the left-hand side of the square as you enter it. You will soon see another of the Cathedral's grand doors on your left, oddly boxed in by shops and bars. There is a statue of Mary and Child on the corner of one of the shops.

Mary and Child

This statue is unusual because it is much gentler and less colourful than most you will see on Antwerp's streets. Also, Mary is usually portrayed as holding baby Jesus, but in this one he is standing on his own two feet. There is still a snake slithering about beneath them.

Map 1.3 - With the cathedral door and Mary behind you, walk into Groenplaats.

Groenplaats

The square is not actually green now, but it was originally the Cathedral cemetery until the eighteenth century and it sat behind the Cathedral grounds wall. Anyone who couldn't afford a tomb in the Cathedral itself ended up here.

Emperor Joseph II was the emperor of Austria which ruled Antwerp in the eighteenth century. He decided that having a cemetery within the city walls was unhealthy, so he declared it illegal and the cemetery was evicted.

For some time the vacated cemetery remained grassy. When Napoleon became Emperor and took control of Antwerp he had the cathedral grounds wall torn down. The ex-cemetery was called Place Bonaparte and planted with lime trees. However it later fell into decline, and when the age of the car arrived it became a car-park.

The square was revamped in the nineties by moving the cars underground and renovating the buildings which surround it. It's now a very nice square with a statue of Rubens holding central position.

Rubens

This statue was commissioned in 1840 to commemorate the bicentenary of the death of Rubens. The sculptor was local artist Willem Geefs.

Rubens stands with his sword at his waist and is dressed very fashionably. The only clue that he is an artist and not some sort of statesman or aristocrat is the painter's palette lying at his feet. The original plan was to have the pedestal decorated with scenes of all his talents, painting, sculpture, engraving, and architecture; however funds ran out so the pedestal is left bare.

Hilton

Stand face to face with Rubens and look right to find the Hilton Hotel occupying a rather grand building.

It was built in the nineteenth century as a hotel and café, but was later turned into a huge department store called the "Grand Bazar du Bon Marché" by Alphonse Kileman who came from Paris. You can see the words "Grand Bazar" inscribed in the stonework to the left of the dome.

The Germans bombed this area in World War I but fortunately they missed the department store. After the war the Kileman family reopened and expanded the store. In the nineties the Hilton moved in.

Map 1.4 - Just to the right of the Hilton hotel stands the Karbonkel Huis - what a wonderful name! Make your way over to it.

Karbonkel Huis

Karbonkel means "diamond" and if you look at the bottom of the pillars on the façade you will see some diamond-head shaped stonework.

At one time a lot of the façade was covered in "karbonkels" but sadly they have been removed and we are only left with a few. Above the diamond-heads are some long-legged birds, flamingoes perhaps. The rest of the columns are covered in intricate stonework.

The Karbonkel Huis used to be one of Antwerp's Grand Cafes. In recent times various businesses have moved in but then moved out and at the time of writing it is awaiting a new owner.

Map 1.5 - Stand between the Hilton and the Karbonkel huis and face away from them. Cross the square and leave it by little Zwaluwstraat which lies on the opposite side of the square.

Map 1.6 - At the end of Zwaluwstraat turn right into Oude Koornmarkt. This is an old cobbled street where the grain market used to take place. Follow this street as it bends to the left.

Pass Papenstraatje on your right and a few steps more will bring you to De Grote Gans on your left at number 38.

De Grote Gans

The Hanseatic League was a powerful confederation of German cities that controlled trade and shipping all around the Baltic Sea for centuries, so you can imagine how important it was to Antwerp to have them in town.

The Big Goose was an inn where visiting members of the Hanseatic League stayed when in town for business. Behind what was once a lovely arcaded façade ran a long courtyard with guestrooms all round it.

In 1923 the then owners thought it would be a great idea to turn the courtyard into a garage and replace the original façade with an ugly garage door. All we have left today is the lovely rococo building to the left of the ugly garage door. It has a lovey iron balcony and at the top a weathervane.

Map 1.7 - Continue along Oude Koornmarkt to reach Pelgrimstraat on your left.

Virgin Mary and Streetlight

On the corner of Pelgrimstraat you will find another Virgin Mary and Child with accompanying streetlight.

This one was removed while the French were in power but was put back up once they had been kicked out.

The Virgin Mary carries a sceptre. Around her are golden stars and above her hovers a dove. The streetlight is decorated with a Mariamonogram – an entwinement of the initials V and M.

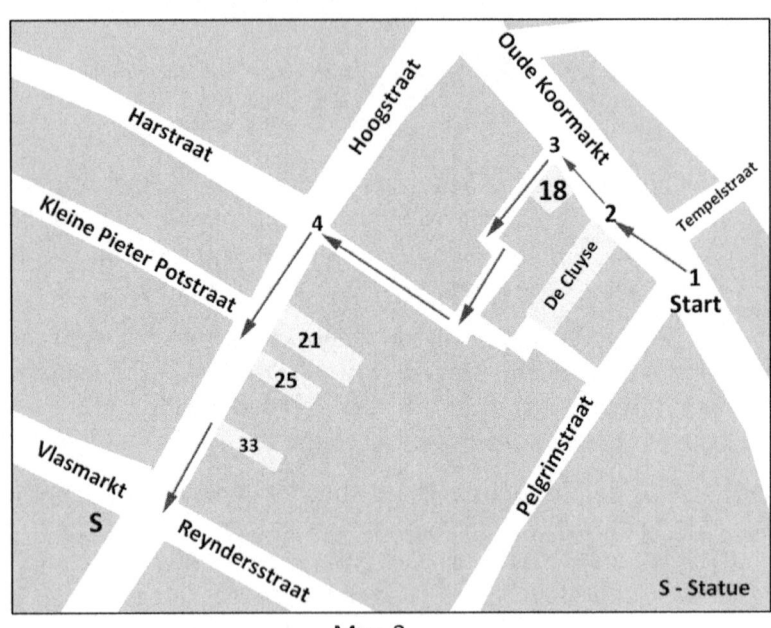

Map 2

Map 2.1 Continue along Oude Koornmarkt to reach number 26 on your left which is called De Cluyse.

De Cluyse

De Cluyse was built in the fourteenth century and was later given by Antwerp to the Hanseatic League to use as an office – a strategic move to keep the lucrative trade business in Antwerp. The League used it for over 100 years – it was very handy as it is just a short walk from the Grote Gans.

Look up to see the eye-catching trefoil stonework around the upper windows - trefoil means three-leaved.

Map 2.2 - Continue along Oude Koornmarkt to find de Gulden Bock at number 18 on your left – it has a marvellous engraving of a goat above the door.

Map 2.3 - Just next door at number 16 is a little alleyway – go through it to reach Vlaeykensgang.

Vlaeykensgang

You will feel as though you have stepped back in time as you walk through this narrow picturesque alley.

Antwerp used to have many alleys like this one, and in those days they were packed with the poorest members of society. Life was hard with poor sanitation and little comfort for anyone. The people who lived and worked in this particular alley were mostly shoemakers.

The alley was scheduled for the bulldozer but it was saved and renovated by a philanthropist called Axel Vervoordt, who clearly loved old things. Nowadays it is home to antique shops, restaurants, and bars.

Follow the alley as it twists and turns, always keeping to the right-hand side wall. You will eventually emerge onto Hoogstraat 15 through another old doorway.

Note – if you find the exit locked and cannot reach Hoogstaat, return to the entranceway and stand with the entranceway behind you.

From there turn left to walk along along Oude Koornmarkt and then turn left again into Hoogstraat. Number 15 is just a few doors down on your left.

Map 2.4 – You will exit Vlaeykensgang at Hoogstraat 15. With the exit behind you turn left to walk along Hoogstraat.

Hoogstraat

Sadly a fire broke out here in 1443 and most of the old buildings on this old street were destroyed. Their replacements were built in a wide variety of styles over the centuries.

An important cloth market was held in this street in the sixteenth century. **Hoogstraat 21 (left hand side)**

Here you find another wonderful gateway made of bluestone. It frames a decorated wooden door with inbuilt ironwork. A handy boot scraper stands on either side of the door down at ground level.

Hoogstraat 25 (left hand side)

Look up to see the lovely iron balconies and the sculpted stonework set into the brickwork

Hoogstraat 33 (left hand side)

Here you will find another beautiful balcony near the top.

You will reach a crossroads with Vlasmarkt and Reyndersstraat.

Virgin Mary shrine

This corner has a very colourful Virgin Mary sheltering under a canopy with golden bells. There is a green slithering snake at her feet. Even the street lamp is decorated with golden bells.

Map 3

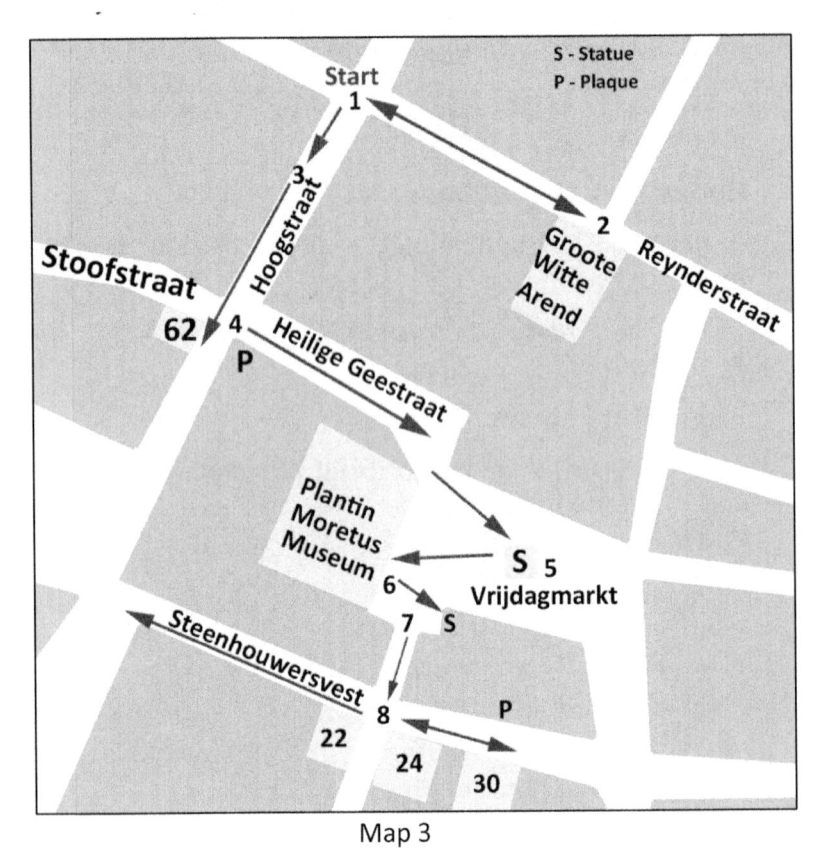

Map 3.1 - Turn left into Reyndersstraat. At number 18 on the right you will find the huge doorway of the Groote Witte Arend.

Groote Witte Arend (Great White Eagle)

The "Groote Witte Arend" building was first documented in 1554. It became a convent in 1660 when its owner gifted it to the church.

It was later sold off to one of Antwerp's merchant families and was used for a variety of industries over the centuries, including, it is said, counterfeiting!

It resumed as a religious community in 1901 when the Daughters of Charity bought it, but it was sold again in 1976. However at least by that time it had gained "protected building" status, so any future owners could not pull it apart as happened to De Cluyse when it was turned into a garage.

It was until recently an interesting stop for lunch or a drink with traditional Belgian meals and beers being sold. However at the time of writing it has closed once more. Hopefully when you visit it will have opened its doors again.

If you do manage to get in, take a look at the old chapel - it's on the far right hand corner as you enter the courtyard.

Map 3.2 - When you want to move on, stand with the Groote Witte Arend door behind you. Turn left to retrace your steps along Reyndersstraat.

When you reach the crossroads turn left into Hoogstraat once more.

Map 3.3 - Walk along Hoogstraat to reach a crossroads with Stoofstraat and Heillige Geestraat. Walk over the crossroads staying on Hoogstraat, but stop immediately at number 62 on your right.

Carpenter's Guild House

This used to be the Carpenter's guild house, and on the facade you can see some carvings showing events from the life of the most famous carpenter of them all, Joseph. They show his marriage to the Virgin Mary, their flight into Egypt to escape Herod, and you can see Jesus helping Dad in the family workshop.

Map 3.4 - Stand at the crossroads with Stoofstraat on your left and Heilige Geeststraat on your right.

Turn right to walk along Heilige Geeststraat. Look up at the corner as you enter Heilig Geeststraat and you will see two engraved plaques.

Poetry Wall

Antwerp has created several Poetry Walls, each one holding the words of a poet or musician who came from Antwerp.

This one holds the lyrics of "De Zwerver", a song by Wannes Van de Velde chosen about a homeless person. The building the plaques are attached to is the café 't Half Souke where Wannes often performed.

Continue along Heilige Geeststraat to enter a square called Vrijdagmarkt which holds a statue of St Catherine.

Vrijdagmarkt

This is where the Friday antique flea market is held. It started in the sixteenth century and was where second hand clothes were bought and sold – a common practise in those days when clothes were a much bigger investment than they are today. The square was blasted in 1945 when a German V bomb hit it, however it was restored. It's still used to sell second hand goods. If it's in full swing when you get there you might be lucky and find a bargain.

The statue in the middle is Saint Catherine, appropriately the patron saint of old cloth buyers. She is shown with a broken wheel at her feet.

She lived in Alexandria in Egypt and tried to convert the local emperor to Christianity. He was not convinced and decided instead to propose to her. Catherine was very religious and turned him down as she would have to give up her faith and start worshipping the local gods. The Emperor responded by trying to torture her. She was to be tied to a wheel and be bludgeoned to death. However, when Catherine touched the wheel it immediately broke in two. That act of God didn't save her though as she was beheaded, but at least that was a quick death. The statue was blown up by bombing in 1945, so this is a replacement.

Map 3.5 - Stand face to face with Saint Catherine and behind her you will see the Plantin-Moretus Museum. Make your way towards it.

Plantin-Moretus Museum

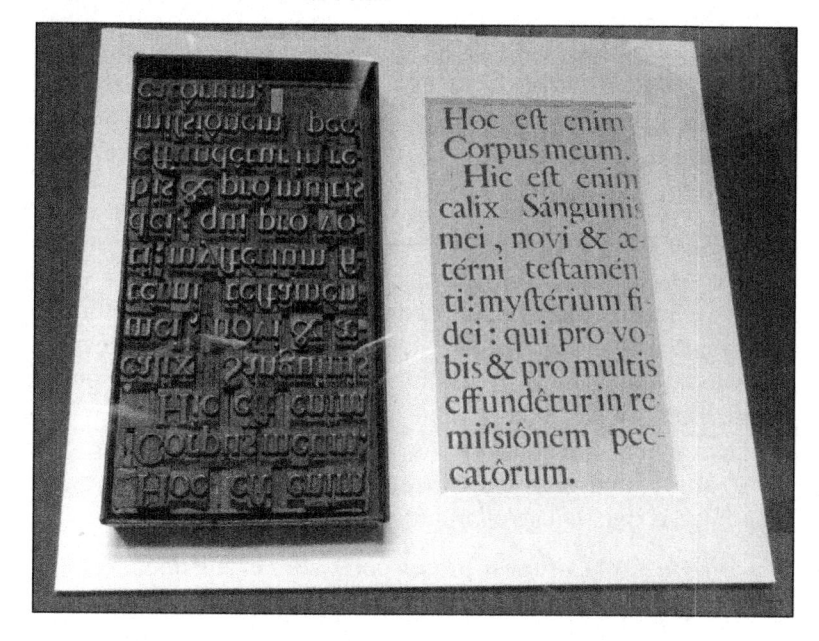

You may have already read about the wealthy Plantin family when exploring the cathedral – they commissioned The Resurrection Triptych by Rubens.

In the sixteenth century The Officina Plantiniana was founded by Christoffel Plantin in Antwerp. He hailed from France but moved to prosperous Antwerp to set up a printing business.

It was a good choice, as by the mid sixteenth century Antwerp had over a hundred printers and booksellers. They sent books out across Europe and Antwerp became the hub of publishing in Northern Europe.

Christopher Plantin is regarded as probably the most important publisher in the sixteenth century.

His family continued the business after his death, maintaining and improving both the business and living premises. In fact the business continued printing until 1866. By then printing had moved into a more modern technical age and the family business couldn't adapt. The family sold the buildings and their contents to Antwerp who turned it into this Museum of Printing.

You can explore both the working rooms and the family accommodation – all lovingly restored. The family clearly were wealthy given the luxurious furnishings – including works of art by Flemish artists of the day. The museum also holds some incredibly rare and valuable books including a Guttenberg bible, and a polyglotta, a bible in five languages. You can also see the two oldest printing presses in the world and the museum has a beautiful courtyard which is worth a stroll through.

Map 3.6 - Exit the museum and pause at the door.

Mary Praying

Take a moment to look at the tiny little statue of Mary praying which sits on the corner of the building opposite the Museum door. It's very unlike the other statues you see dotted around town.

Map 3.7 - Turn right to leave the square by Vrijdagmarktstraatje. You will reach a crossroads with Steenhouwersvest.

Two little gabled houses sit on the corners of Korte Riddersstraat opposite you.

Den Dondercloot and the Red Cat

On the right-hand corner at number 22 is another Virgin Mary shrine. Mary stands beneath a canopy with a gilded halo and a dove. Baby Jesus is carrying an apple.

The house she is attached to has a plaque above the door with two little angels hugging a cannonball, and beneath them is inscribed Den DonderCloot – The Cannonball.

The other little gabled house at number 24 has what looks a bit like a red cat above the door, but no clue why.

Map 3.8 - You could now stop for some refreshment. If that doesn't appeal to you, face the gable houses and turn right along Steenhouwersvest. Continue from "Towards the River" on page 78.

Otherwise if you like the idea of some hot chocolate and a bit of a rest, turn left along Steenhouwersvest. You will soon reach Gunther Watte just a few doors down at number 30 on the right – it's renowned for wonderful hot chocolate.

When you exit the chocolate shop turn left to return to the Den DonderCloot crossroads. Continue straight ahead along Steenhouwersvest.

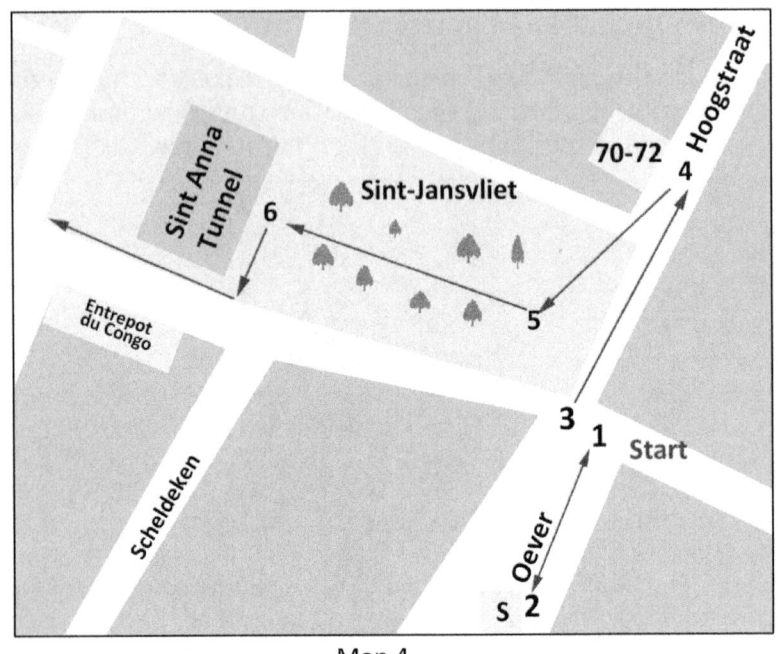

Map 4

Towards the River

Map 4.1 - You will reach the corner of Oever on your left. Take a walk down Oever to see the statue of Jacob Jordaens.

Jacob Jordaens

He is the third of the most famous three Painters from Antwerp; Rubens, Van Dyke, and Jacob Jordaens

He was very different from the other two artists who both travelled extensively. He was also indifferent to

Italian painting unlike his contemporaries who studied the Italian masters. Jordaens more or less stayed in Antwerp his entire life. It didn't seem to do him any harm as he was a very successful artist.

He was the artist who painted "The Education of Jupiter" which you might have seen if you visited the Rockoxhuis museum. He is also well known for his group scenes which illustrate life in Antwerp, with its drinking, partying, and general joie de vivre.

He worked with Rubens on occasion and was influenced by him. You might spot a similarity between his and Rubens's ladies in biblical or mythological scenes; they are usually on the plump side.

Map 4.2 - Backtrack along Oever. At its end you will see a tree filled square called Sint-Jansvliet.

Map 4.3 - Enter the square. Keep the trees on your left-hand side and walk along the side of the square. You will walk into Hoogstraat once more.

Just a few steps along Hoogstraat will bring you to number 70-72 on your left. It's a very obvious old red brick building which has an unusual sculpture above the doorway and a splendid old pump to the right of the door.

Black Panther Gallery

This is now the Black Panther gallery, Antwerp's oldest art gallery.

Originally in the early fourteenth century it was the Sint-Julianusgasthuis, an inn for pilgrims passing through Antwerp on their way to or from Rome. A few centuries later a chapel was added to it, and another couple of centuries passed before it became a hospital.

Even today as an art gallery it still has one religious connection; by tradition every year on Holy Thursday a

Pilgrim's table is placed inside, and twelve local poor people are served a meal.

If the doorway is open, pop in for a look at the lovely courtyard.

Map 4.4 - Retrace your steps along Hoogstraat to return to Sint-Jansvliet.

Sint-Jansvliet

This square used to be part of a canal for small barges which joined the river just a short distance away. The canal was filled in in 1882. It got its name from Sint-Janspoort, the city gate which used to stand here.

The square's main feature now is the building which stands alone near the river, and which gives access to the Sint-Anna Tunnel.

Map 4.5 - Walk through the trees on the square to reach the tunnel entrance building.

Now you have a choice. You can take a walk through the Sint-Anna Tunnel to reach the other side of the river. The walk will take you about fifteen minutes each way.

If you prefer to skip this part of the walk, continue from "Along the Riverside" on page 82.

Through the Sint-Annatunnel

The tunnel runs under the river to the other side and is for both pedestrians and cyclists. It was finally built in 1933 along with a car tunnel to join the two halves of the city; it had been needed for years. When it was opened Antwerp had a grand party on both banks of the river, with the Royal Family and many dignitaries present.

The entrance on the other side of the Scheldt was blown up by the Germans in WWII, and until it was reconstructed the locals had to resort to ferries.

The tunnel is still well-used by the locals, and it's fun to do. You still ride down thirty-one metres on the original wooden escalators to the tunnel.

On the other bank

If you walk through the tunnel, you will get a view of Antwerp from the other side of the river, but to be honest there is not much else to do.

If you face the river and turn left to walk along Lode Zielenslaan, you will reach Frederik van Eedenplein which is full of odd statues and old war memorabilia.

When you have had enough, return through the tunnel to Sint Jansvliet.

Along the Riverside

Map 4.6 - Stand facing the door of the tunnel entrance building and turn left to walk around it.

As you do you will see a large building on your left, with Entrepot du Congo written high on the façade.

Entrepot du Congo

Belgium ruled the Belgian Congo until 1960 when it gained independence and became the Democratic Republic of the Congo.

This was one of the trade buildings where the valuable ivory, rubber, coffee, and cocoa cargoes from The Congo were stored. They were unloaded from the ships which docked on the river just across the road.

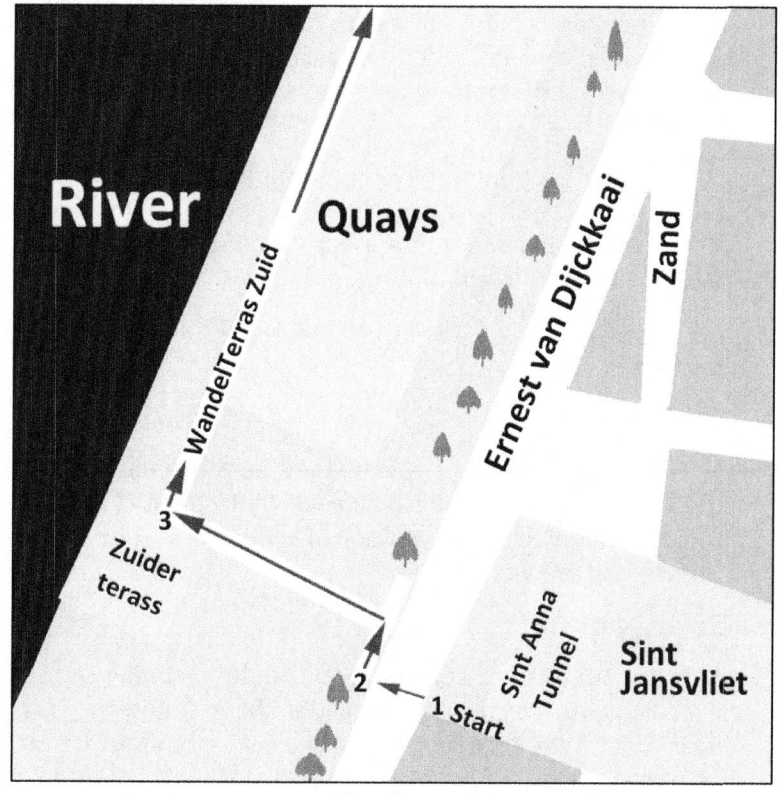

Map 5

Map 5.1 - Carefully cross the main road by the zebra crossing.

Map 5.2 - Climb the stairs to reach the WandelTerras Zuid, the South River Terrace.

Look to your right to see a long line of sheds with intricate ironwork roofs running along the riverside.

The Old River Quays

It was Napoleon who had Antwerp's first quay built but many more followed, and by the time of World War I Antwerp was one of the world's busiest ports. This is where the goods from Antwerp's far-flung trading partners were loaded and unloaded. It was a hive of activity, and these were the sheds where the goods in transit were stored.

After the war, huge locks were built on the Scheldt to allow container ships to reach the new docks which were built further north on the river, leaving the old quays behind and abandoned.

As you approach the river you will see The Zuiderterass on your left.

Zuiderterass

The original pavilion which stood here burned down in 1973 and this is its modern replacement. It's a restaurant and the windows run from floor to ceiling so it gives diners an excellent view of the river.

River Walkway

In the nineteenth century, you couldn't actually see the river from Antwerp because of the sheds lining the busy river front. So this raised walkway was built to let the locals see their river again.

At the time of writing there are plans to add some greenery to the walkway which will make it a much prettier stroll.

Map 5.3 - Follow the walkway as it turns right to walk above the riverside.

Map 6

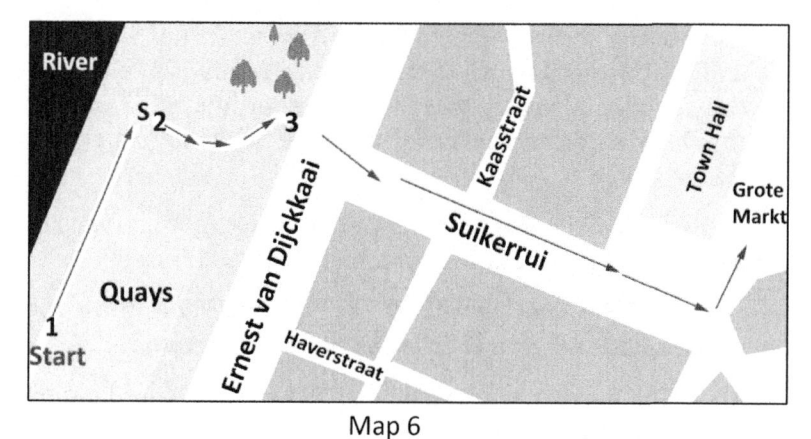

Map 6.1 - Continue until you reach the statue of Minerva.

Minerva

This statue is by a famous Italian sculptor, Marcello Macherini.

Minerva faces north towards Antwerp's bustling port and she also has another connection to Antwerp. She was the logo of a luxury brand of cars produced locally in Antwerp between the wars; they are valuable collector's items now.

Rolls of Rolls Royce fame, was a dealer in Minerva cars before he went into the automobile business himself.

Map 6.2 - Continue along the walkway and down the curving slope which is lined with decorative lanterns.

At the bottom of the slope you will see two lions holding the coat of arms of Antwerp. You also get a very good view of the Cathedral tower.

Map 6.3 - Cross the road carefully. Walk straight up Suikerrui towards the cathedral. When you reach the end of Suikerrui, turn left to return to the Grote Markt where this walk ends.

If you have time and energy you could start Walk 3.

Walk 3 – The Castle and St Pauls (1.6 km)

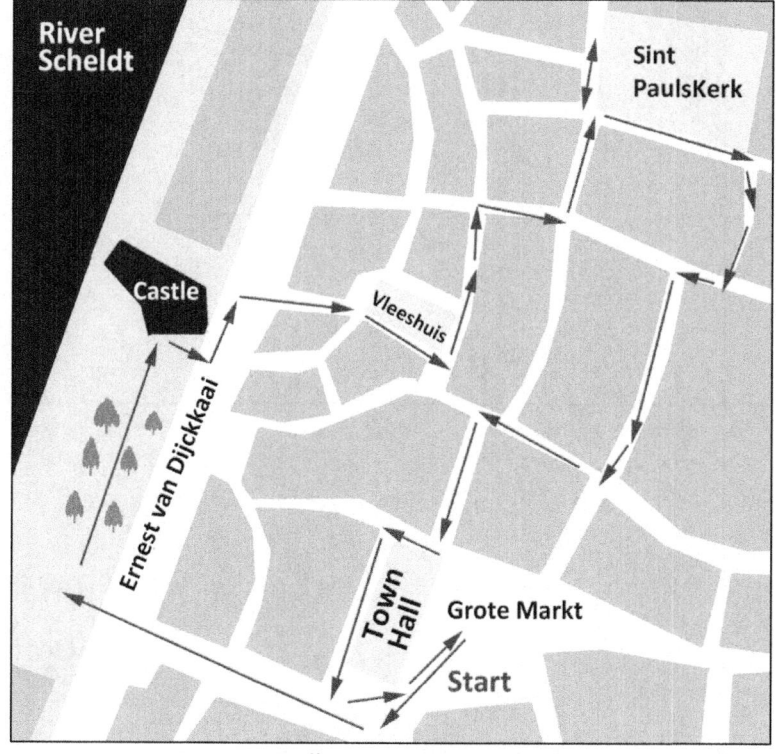

Walk 3 Overview

This walk takes you down to the riverside and to the castle. Then through the oldest part of Antwerp and out to the lovely Saint Paul's Church, before heading back to the Grote Markt.

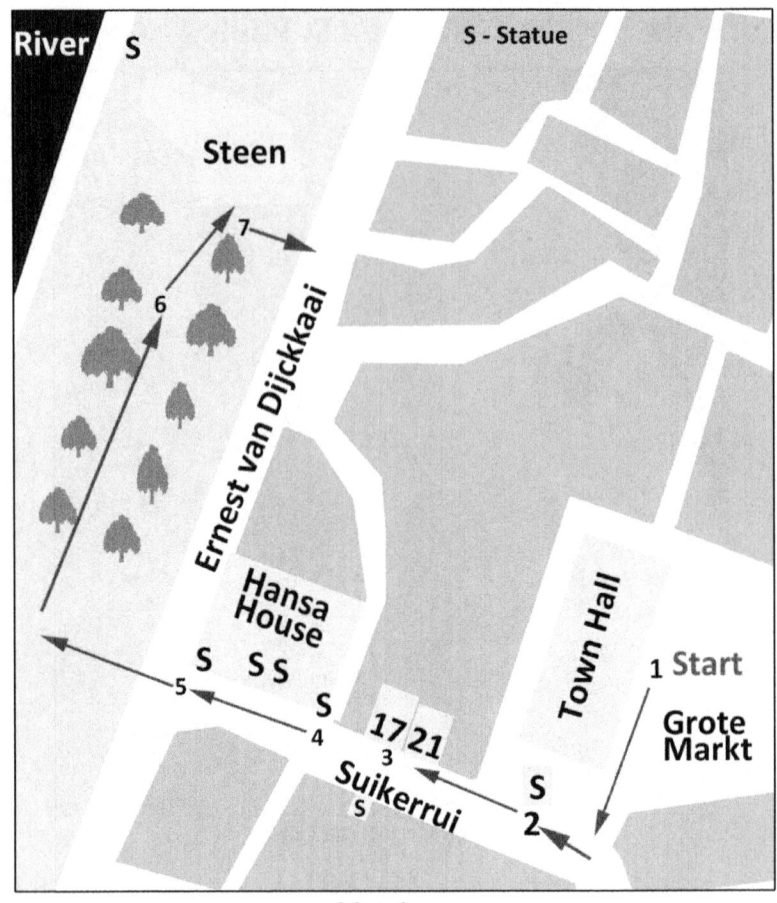

Map 1

This walk starts in Grote Markt.

Map 1.1 - Stand facing the Town Hall and turn left to walk along the front of the building. Turn right to walk into Suikerrui.

Suikerrui

Suikerrui is a very old street and was originally part of the moat which ran round the city wall in the middle ages.

So it was firstly used for defence and later for transport, but finally it became the city sewer. At one point there were three bridges crossing it.

The Docker

ARBEID
VRIJHEID

On a little square at the start of the street you will see a statue of a débardeur – a docker. It represents the toils of the workers who handled the huge cargoes arriving at Antwerp's quays. The original statue is in Paris where it was displayed in 1885. The critics loved it and raved about it –

> Never has such tragic and touching expression,
> such energy, oppression, suffering and resignation,
> been put into a figure, with such intensity.

Map 1.2 - Continue down Suikerrui to reach number 21 on your right.

Ruien

In the sixteenth century the city fathers decided to cover the canals/sewers up on health grounds – however it was up to each citizen to cover up his bit. That was an expensive task so how it was done depended on how wealthy each citizen was. The wealthy used stone, the less fortunate used brick.

The sewers were still in use until the 1990s when they were drained and emptied. They suddenly became a tourist attraction and in 2004 they were opened up to the public – letting you see not just the canals but the remains of old Antwerp which is buried below today's city. This is where the tours are booked and start from.

Be warned – it's still a bit pungent and there are lots of insects down there – so decide how brave you are before you commit. It takes a couple of hours to complete. Also if it starts to rain you will have to make a very quick exit! They do kit you out in rubber boots and trousers. If you are interested and haven't pre-booked a slot already, you could pop in and check out the next available tour

Just next door at number 17 is the Diamond Museum.

DIVA – The Diamond Museum

Since Antwerp is a major centre of the world diamond market it's not surprising to find a diamond museum, although it's not in the Diamond District which might have been more appropriate.

The building the museum sits in is actually the old Police Office which was built in 1880. Downstairs was the police station and upstairs was where the Chief Constable lived.

Diva also incorporates the silver museum, so you will find more silver on display than diamonds which might be a bit disappointing to visitors looking for lots of sparklers. However if jewellery is interesting to you and you have time you could pay a visit.

Just opposite Diva at number 18 is a rather ugly building, but it does have a small but lovely statue of the Virgin Mary and Jesus on the second floor.

Map 1.3 - Continue down Suikerrui passing Kaasstraat on your right. The next building on your right is the "Hansa House".

Hansa House

As already mentioned, The Hanseatic League was an alliance of Northern Europe's wealthiest port cities, mostly German. With trade expanding the League commissioned this huge building and moved out of their original office in De Cluyse which you saw on Walk 2. The merchants from Germany could stay here and it also gave them a safe location to stash their merchandise.

The building is decorated with some interesting statues representing the rivers which the Hanseatic League cities stood on. High above you are two old men with beards who represent the Rhine and the Scheldt.

There are also two female statues which represent the Elbe and the Weser. Popular legend says that the sculptor, Lambeaux, used his girlfriends as models. He also sculpted Brabo on the Grote Markt which you saw earlier.

Map 1.4 - Continue to the end of Suikerrui.

Map 1.5 - Carefully cross the main road and then turn right to walk through the trees and along the riverside to reach the castle.

Het Steen – The Stone

Where the castle stands is a bit off the usual tourist track, but this used to be a bustling neighbourhood hosting the fish market.

This castle is what is left of Antwerp's oldest building. It was called The Stone because at that time most buildings where wooden, so a stone castle was something very much out of the ordinary.

The castle was a prison for a couple of hundred years, and as such was frequently attacked by the locals because of the unfairness of the justice meted out there. Those inmates who could afford it were given comfortable rooms with a riverside view and lived very nicely. The poor suffered torture and lived in horrific conditions and frequently died from disease caught there.

The castle is now much, much smaller than it was originally. In fact Antwerp carried out the wholesale demolition of this entire neighbourhood in the name of progress. Antwerp needed the harbour and the docks much more than the quaint buildings which were to be found here. The castle was saved from total demolition by a single council vote – although they still flattened most of it and moved what was left further down the river out of the way. Perhaps they regret that now.

Outside the castle stands the statue of Lange Wapper. He was a magical water-being who could make himself as tiny as a baby, or so huge that he could walk from one town to another in just one step. He loved to tease the children and frighten any passing drunks.

He also liked the ladies; one legend tells us that he liked to turn himself into a baby lying on the beach as a pretty mother passed by. She of course would rescue the baby, whereupon Lange Wapper would instantly grow to a full man. You would think they would have learned not to pick up abandoned babies on the beach!

Map 1.6 - Walk towards the castle entrance and climb the ramp.

Stand in front of the main gate and look above it. You will spot a rather faded Semini, a Scandinavian god of fertility from the second century.

He originally had a prodigious manhood, which the local women would appeal to and touch when trying to conceive. However the prudish Jesuits chopped it off in the seventeenth century. The people of Antwerp still call themselves "Semini's children".

Enter the little courtyard. On your right you will pass a crucifix which has stood since the castle was a prison. This was where those heading for the noose said their final prayers. The castle became an archaeological museum in the nineteenth century, but currently lies unused.

Walk through what's left of the castle to reach the river walkway again. As you do, you will find some war memorials.

War Memorials

Royal Hamilton Light Infantry

You will pass a war memorial and a plaque commemorating the actions of the Royal Hamilton Light Infantry in 1944.

As you read on Walk 1, the Germans held the port and the River access even after Antwerp had been liberated. It fell to the Canadians and the Belgian resistance to battle with the German Army to free the vital port area of Antwerp, as the Allies desperately needed a port to get supplies in quickly.

Once the port was secure they then fought upriver to free the River Scheldt which was still in German hands - with a huge loss of life in the Canadian army. They succeeded and fittingly it was a Canadian ship which brought the first supplies up the Scheldt and into the port of Antwerp.

Harry

There is another plaque here dedicated to Eugène Colson. He was a leader of the Belgian Resistance who was known as "Harry". He led the Resistance to fight side by side with the Canadian Army to liberate Antwerp's port.

War Memorial Statue

There is also a statue at the entrance to the river walkway. It reads:

> Aan allen die zich verzet hebben en streden
> voor de bevrijding van Antwerpen

Which translates as:

> As a tribute to all who fought
> for the liberation of Antwerp

If you look further along the river you will see the bustling new docks which are now second only in size to Rotterdam. You might want to take a little walk along the walkway and then return to this point to continue.

Make your way back through the castle to the exit and walk down the ramp.

Map 1.7 - Turn left to reach the main road.

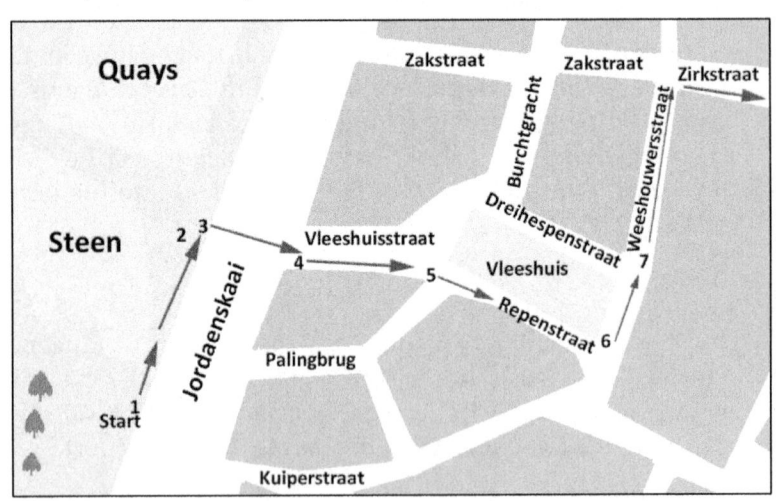

Map 2

Map 2.1 - Turn left to walk along the side of the Castle on Jordaenskaai.

The Original Castle Wall

As you pass alongside the castle look for the wall section which is made of a very old dark stone and is quite different from the rest of the castle. That's the original castle wall – the rest is part of a facelift the castle got in the sixteenth century.

Map 2.2 - Stop when you reach the end of the castle.

Old Boats

Ahead of you is another line of old quayside buildings. At the time of writing they house a collection of old boats in the Maritime museum which you could visit.

Map 2.3 - Stand at the kerbside of Jordaenskaai. Look across it and along Vleeshuisstraat to see the lovely castle-like Vleeshuis.

Cross the main road carefully and take a few steps into Vleeshuisstraat.

Helvetia Huis

The first building on your left is called the Helveitia Huis. It was built for a Swiss shipping company which transported emigrants from Europe to the USA and South America in the nineteenth century. Take a few steps into Vleeshuisstraat to see a wonderful frieze above the first floor corner window. It's full of dolphins and seagulls – very fitting for a shipping company. Above the frieze is a sweet little tower.

Map 2.4 - Continue down Vleeshuisstraat towards the Vleeshuis.

The Castle Wall

You are now in the oldest part of the old town. You can see what remains of the thirteenth century wall which guarded the castle on both sides of the road as you approach the Vleeshuis.

There is some paving crossing the street which shows where the wall would have run to join both halves up. The wall was about 1.3 metres thick, about 12 metres high, and guarded by towers.

Vleeshuis

The Vleeshuis is over 500 years old. The first building on this site was a meat market, and was the only place where meat could be sold in Antwerp. When Antwerp became a thriving and expanding city, the butcher's guild decided a larger hall was needed. So this gothic building was constructed over the old market in the sixteenth century. It's quite striking with its layers of red and white bricks – a style appropriately known as Bacon Layers.

Inside there is a huge sales hall which had 62 stalls which the butchers could use to sell their produce.

At one point the building was used for wine storage, but is now a museum of music – more interesting than it sounds.

Map 2.5 - Walk along the right hand side of the Vleeshuis, climbing some steps on Repenstraat. Turn left at the top of the steps to reach the museum entrance on Weeshouwersstraat.

Vleeshuis Museum of Music

If you have arrived Thursday to Sunday the museum will be open, but unfortunately at the time or writing, it is shut the rest of the week. If you do manage to get in, make sure you follow the audio guide to enjoy and understand what you are seeing.

Don't miss seeing "Orida", an ancient bell which was cast in the early fourteenth century and which used to hang in the Cathedral bell tower. It rang out when disaster threatened Antwerp and it is inscribed with the ominous words:

> Orida vocor
> I am called the Terrible One

***Map 2.6** - When you exit the museum, stand with the museum door behind you and turn left.*

***Map 2.7** - Pass Driehespenstraat on your left and you will reach a crossroads with Zakstraat and Zirkstraat. Turn right into Zirkstraat.*

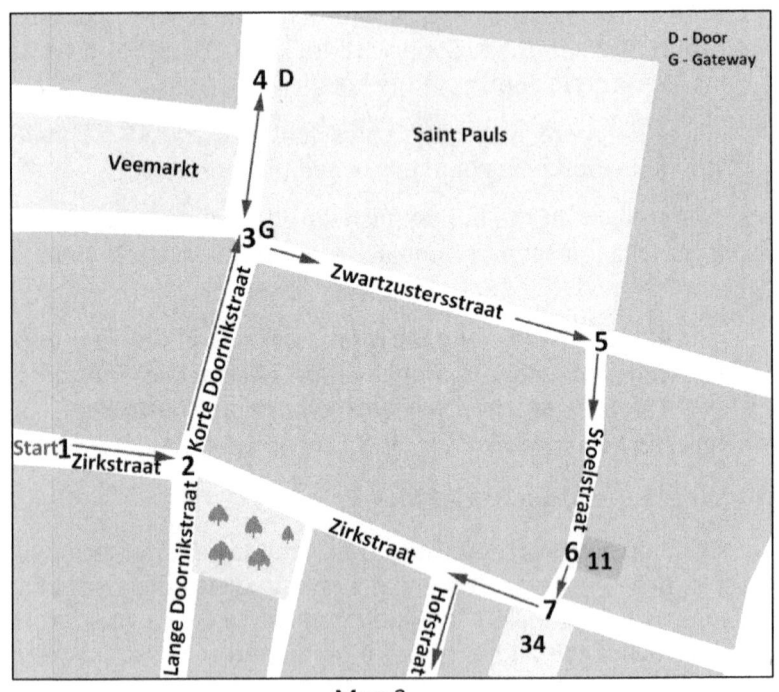

Map 3

***Map 3.1** - Walk along Zirkstraat and you will reach a crossroads with Korte Doornikstraat and Lange Doornikstraat.*

The next destination is Saint Paul's church which is well worth visiting and it's free. However at the time of writing, it is only open in the afternoons between 14:00 and 17:00 from April 1st to October 31st.

If the time is not right you may as well skip this section by walking over the crossroads in front of you, and then taking the next right which is Hofstraat. Pick the route up from "Highest Point in Antwerp" on page 106.

Map 3.2 - Otherwise to reach the church, turn left into Korte Doornikstraat.

As you walk down this street you will see a beautiful gateway ahead of you – the entrance to Sint-Pauluskerk garden. Inside is the Garden of Calvary which you will visit shortly, as access to it is through the church.

Map 3.3 - Pass the gateway and continue along Veemarkt to the left of the gateway to reach the main church doors.

Belgian Basketball

As you do, you might be surprised to see a basketball field in the middle of the square on your left. Basketball became very popular after World War II thanks to the influence of the American soldiers who were stationed here.

Sint-Pauluskerk

This is one of Antwerp's best churches. It replaced an earlier church which was constantly being flooded, so they rebuilt it on a grander scale and most importantly gave it an elevated floor to safeguard against future floods.

Like many of Antwerp's churches it has suffered both fire and the French. The French stole most of the paintings but they did return them eventually.

Fire struck more than once, the last time in 1968 when the local population turned out in force to save what they could of the interior. They rescued all the paintings and sculptures, and even though it took a long time the church has been rebuilt and restored. Inside you can see the saved works of art.

As you enter you will see a dramatic white interior with contrasting black and white decoration. Make your way over to the left hand wall to find the Mysteries.

Mysteries

The Mysteries consists of a set of fifteen paintings. They basically tell us the story of Mary's life from The Annunciation to the moment she is crowned Queen of Heaven.

The leading artists of Antwerp, led by Rubens, each produced a painting to complement The Madonna of the Rosary by Caravaggio which you will see soon.

The big three are all there. Rubens painted "The Flagellation", Jordaens painted "The Crucifixion", and Van Dyck painted the "Bearing of the Cross".

At the end of the Mysteries you will find Our Lady's Chapel – take a look at the altarpiece.

Madonna of the Rosary – Caravaggio/Quertenmont

The masterpiece by Caravaggio is actually not here but it should be. It was given to St Paul's as a gift from Antwerp's leading artists.

It was later appropriated by Emperor Joseph II of Austria who shipped it to Vienna where it still resides in a museum. So the version you see now is a copy by a local artist called Quertenmont.

There is a popular local belief that the copy was switched with the original before it was removed, and so it now hangs proudly in Vienna and the original Caravaggio is still here. A lovely story and who knows?

The painting is flanked with gorgeous spiralling pillars, spot the little angels dancing, sleeping, and playing musical instruments, surrounded by roses on the twirling spirals.

Now look along the choir to see the dramatic high altar and behind that some lovely stained glass windows.

The Choir

The artists who embellished the choir decorated it with all sorts of interesting figures, from birds nibbling at fruit, to angels having a sing song which is all very cheerful. However if you are a sinner there are as many warnings on what lies ahead. Find the tomb of Ophovius. It has a crying cherub at the top holding an hourglass and a skull – a reminder that time runs out for everyone eventually.

The confessionals are decorated with dogs, lions, fighting cocks, and monkeys, which all represent our bad side. There is also a skeleton, another reminder that we only have so much time - all warning us to repent now, or regret it later.

Garden of Calvary

For many people the highlight of the church is the Garden of Calvary which lies in a little courtyard. To reach it, stand at the main door facing the altar – the entrance to the garden is on your right. It holds 63 statues depicting scenes and characters from the last days of Christ.

You can join a little tour round the church and garden which is run regularly and very informative. Just ask inside.

Map 3.4 - When you leave the church, return to the lovely garden gateway you passed earlier. With it behind you turn left into Zwartzusterstraat.

Map 3.5 - Take the next right into Stoelstraat.

Stoelstraat

At number 11 you will find the only wooden house still existing in Antwerp – even if it's just the façade.

Until the sixteenth century most houses were wooden, but of course fire was always a danger – which is why only this one has survived. After 1546 all new houses had to be made of stone by law. The wall surfaces are actually filled in with woven branches and then plastered with mud. It's been a listed building since 1949.

Map 3.6 – Continue to reach a T-junction with Zirkstraat and in front of you is number 34, De Gulde Handt.

De Gulde Handt

Behind the stone gateway is a courtyard and buildings from the sixteenth century. The building is thought to have once been where salt was traded.

It was owned by several merchants over the centuries, one of which gave the building its current name, The Gilded Hand. The old wooden door is decorated with a hand with the name of the building above it, although the hand is stone grey and not golden. If the gateway is open you can peep into the courtyard.

Map 3.7 - Facing the Guilde Handt, turn right along Zirkstraat and take the first street on the left which is called Hofstraat.

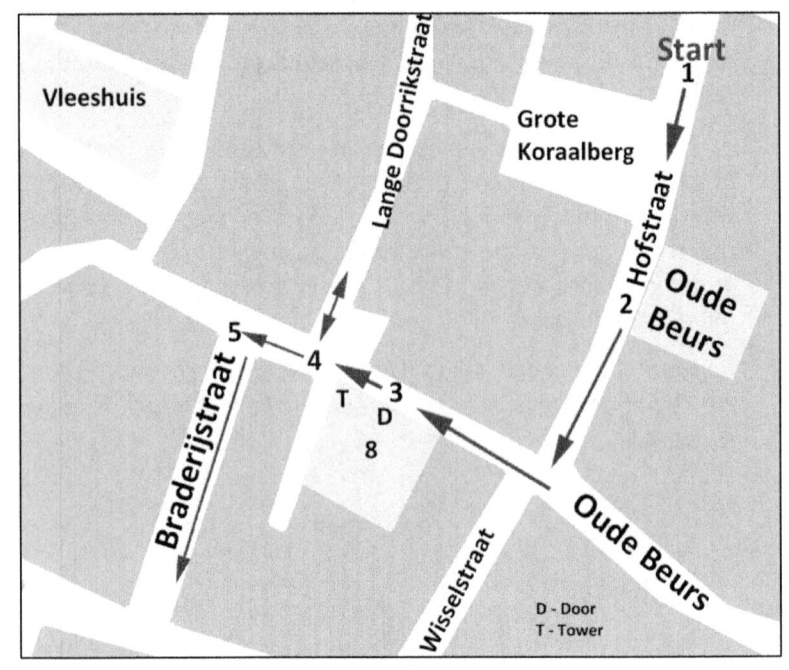

Map 4

Highest point in Antwerp

Map 4.1 - Continue along Hofstraat. You will reach a little square on your right, which is filled with trees and a fountain.

It is called Grote Koraalberg, Big Coral Mountain. On the other side of the square is another small square called Kleine Koraalberg, Little Coral Mountain.

You might have noticed the very slight hill you just climbed on Hofstraat? The two squares got their names because this is said to be one of the highest points in Antwerp!

Just past the square at number 15 on your left you will find an anonymous wooden door. If it's open go inside and through a little passage into a lovely courtyard.

The Oude Beurs

This was where valuable spices and other commodities were once traded, and was effectively the stock exchange until the construction of a purpose built Stock Exchange building. It was in use until 1515. You can enjoy the lovely arcaded courtyard and its dinky watchtower.

The tower is called a Pagaddertorn; pagador is Spanish for paymaster. There used to be 41 Pagaddertorn around Antwerp but now there are just nine standing. In the days when Spain was in power, merchants would send lookouts to the towers attached to their homes to watch for ships coming into harbour. The lookout who spotted and identified a ship first was given a fee, because the merchant could then rush to market and buy up stocks in the ship identified and make a killing.

The rooms at the top of the tower are very cramped, so the lookouts sent up there were all selected for their small stature. Because of their size the children of Antwerp were nicknamed pagadders.

At the time of writing the Oude Beurs building is used as a venue for amateur performance artists, so you might find something on.

Map 4.2 - Exit Oude Beurs and turn left. You will reach a crossroads with the street Oude Beurs.

Turn right along Oude Beurs and you will reach number 8 on your left.

The Mirror

Here you will see another of Antwerp's famous "Spanish Gates". This one is called The Mirror and if you look at the sculpture above the door you will see where the name comes from. A mother is looking in a mirror and can see the reflection of her child.

This street was one of the main streets in medieval Antwerp and this mansion was the family home of one of Antwerp's aristocratic families. However as is often the case, it was sold on to various wealthy individuals, although in 1888 it did become a girl's school.

The courtyard has a pagaddertore. At the time of writing the courtyard is not open to the public, but you might be lucky when you visit and find you can go in to see it.

Map 4.3 - Face The Mirror door and turn right. Walk along to the next junction.

Map 4.4

If you didn't manage to get into the courtyard of the Mirror, you can still get a glimpse of the very top of the pagaddertore.

To do so, turn right down Lange Doornikstraat for about twenty feet. Turn round and look up and you will see just the tip of the Pagaddertore peeping over the nearest roof corner.

Return to Oude Beurs and turn right again.

Map 4.5 - Take the next left, Braderijstraat.

Braderijstraat

Its name roughly translates as Roast Street. Before the destruction of this area by the Spanish Fury this street was full of inns and taverns which served roasted cuts of meat, fresh from the Vleesmarkt which is lies just nearby.

Map 5

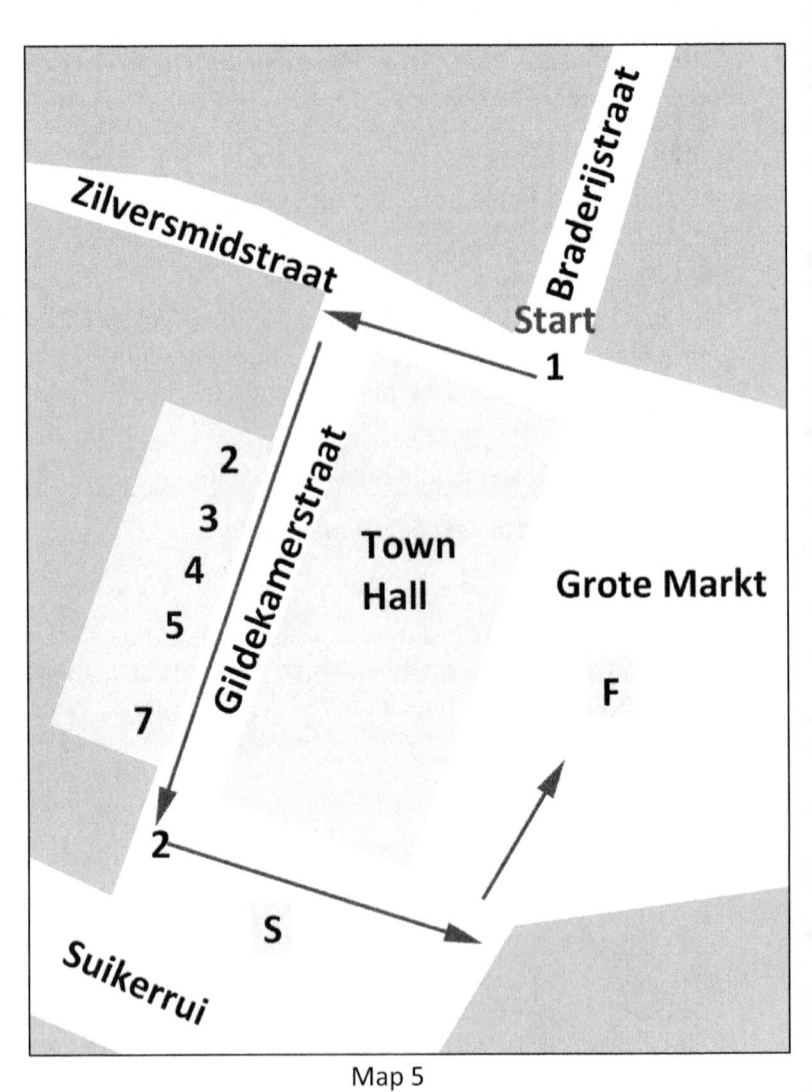

Map 5.1 - At its end, turn right to walk along the side of the Town Hall on Zilversmidstraat. Take the first left into Gildekamersstraat.

Gildekamersstraat

This street was home to several guild-houses, but the original buildings were mostly lost in the Spanish Fury. They were rebuilt but the left-hand side of the street was again demolished as the land was needed to build the Town Hall.

The right-hand side suffered a similar fate when it was decided to build the Folklore Museum, but at least the architects replicated the facades of the original buildings and reinstated the wonderful old Spanish Gates.

De Roose at number 2 was a warehouse and Number 3 was The Archers' guild-house.

Number 4 was called de Vier Winden, The Four Winds, and was The Shippers guild-house. It is especially ornate - if you stand back you can see that the gable is decorated with four heads, one for each of the four winds, North, South, East and West.

Numbers 5 and 7 also have handsome stone gates.

Map 5.2 - When you reach the end of Gildekamersstraat you will find yourself back in Suikerrui again. Turn left to return to the Grote Markt where this walk ends.

Walk 4 – Newer Antwerp and Rubens (2.8 km)

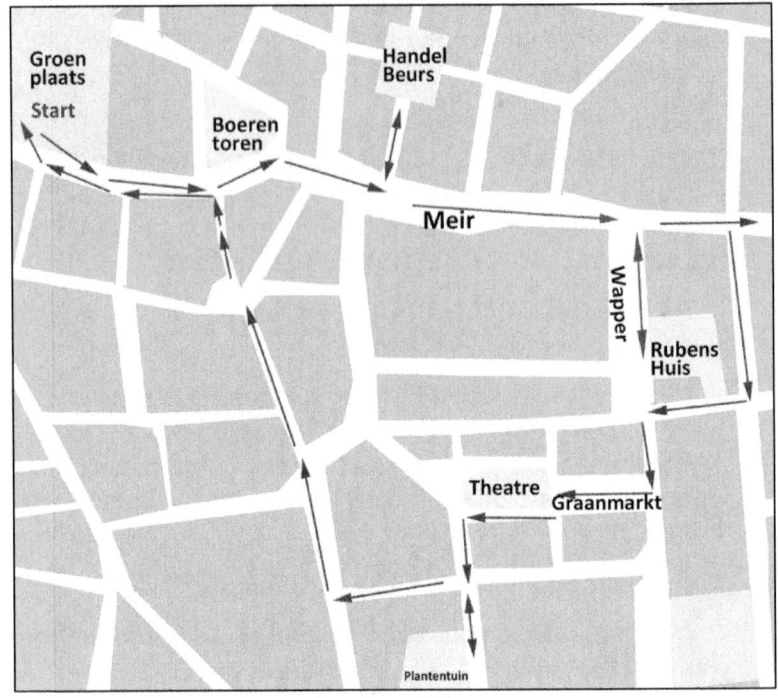

Walk 4 Overview

This walk takes you along Meir, Antwerp's busiest shopping street, to see the palaces and mansions which still line it.

You then head south through the fashion district to reach another marvelous museum, and finaly head back to Groenplats via a little gastronimic corner of Antwerp.

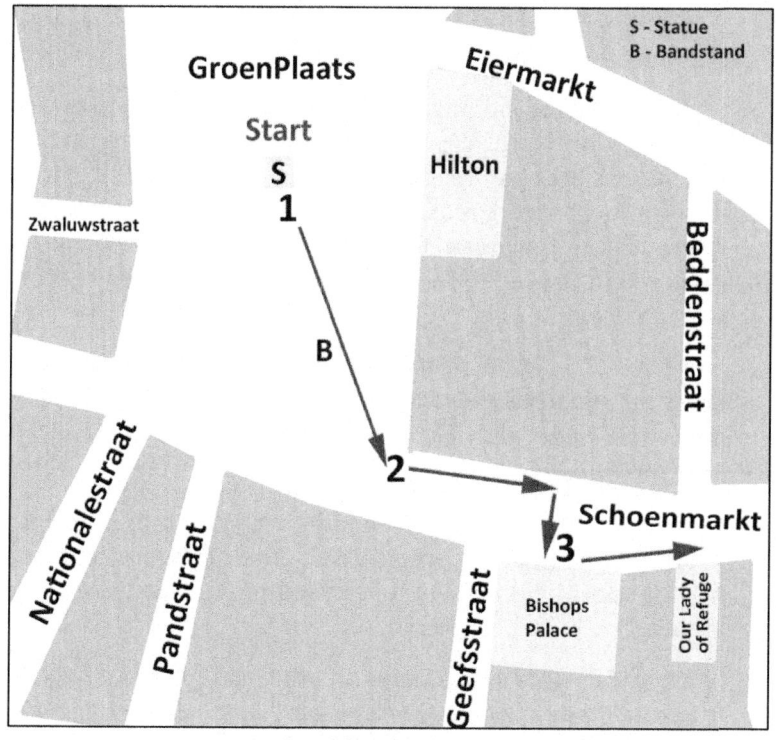

Map 1

This walk starts in Groenplaats, the square which sits on one side of the Cathedral and which you may have already visited on Walk 2.

Make your way to stand beside the statue of Rubens, and then look to the right of the Hilton hotel to see a skyscraper behind it.

Boerentoren

It was the first skyscraper constructed in Europe. When it was designed, the city fathers insisted that it must not obstruct the view of the cathedral. In fact that rule is still in place and keeps old Antwerp from being filled with skyscrapers.

The Boerentoren was the tallest building in Europe until the nineteen fifties.

It was hit by bombs in World War II but its skeleton survived. Antwerp was going to demolish it in the sixties, but it was instead restored and is worth a look. It is decorated in Art Deco style inside and out. It's called Boerentoren (farmer's tower) by the locals because its main resident used to be Kredietbank, a bank whose clients were farmers.

Map 1.1 - Stand facing the same direction as Rubens. Cross the square diagonally left passing a little band-stand to reach the square corner. Leave the square by turning left into Schoenmarkt.

The area on your left hand-side was more or less destroyed by bombs during WWII, and they were replaced by a modern and frankly ugly shopping arcade. So try to ignore it.

Map 1.2 - Pass Geefsstraat on your right and just beyond it you will see a white wall and gateway. Behind it is the Bishop's Palace.

Bishops Palace/Conference Centre

The first religious building was erected on this site in the thirteenth century, and in the sixteenth century it became the bishop's residence.

The palace hidden behind the wall was built in the eighteenth century in a very French style, which is perhaps why it was appropriated by the French as an administrative building when they were in power. It remained an administrative building even after they left.

The Germans moved in during World War I and held trials there, issuing death and hard labour sentences. After the war Antwerp placed a memorial in the chamber where the trials were held, dedicated to those who had suffered its judgements.

The palace was bombed in World War II by a V-2 rocket, but was later reconstructed and remained in government hands. In the nineties a large part of it was turned into a conference centre and a smaller part was returned to its former role as the Bishop's Residence.

Map 1.3 - Walk alongside the wall of the Bishops Palace and reach number 8 where you will see an old church, Our Lady of Refuge.

Our Lady of Refuge

It's made of red brick and has a statue of a crowned Virgin Mary carrying Baby Jesus above the door.

The locals call this church the Little Shoemakers' Chapel because of its location on Schoenmarkt. It's a peaceful little church with fewer tourists than the other churches you have visited. It welcomes everyone and until the seventies it was used by the prostitutes of Antwerp when in need of a prayer.

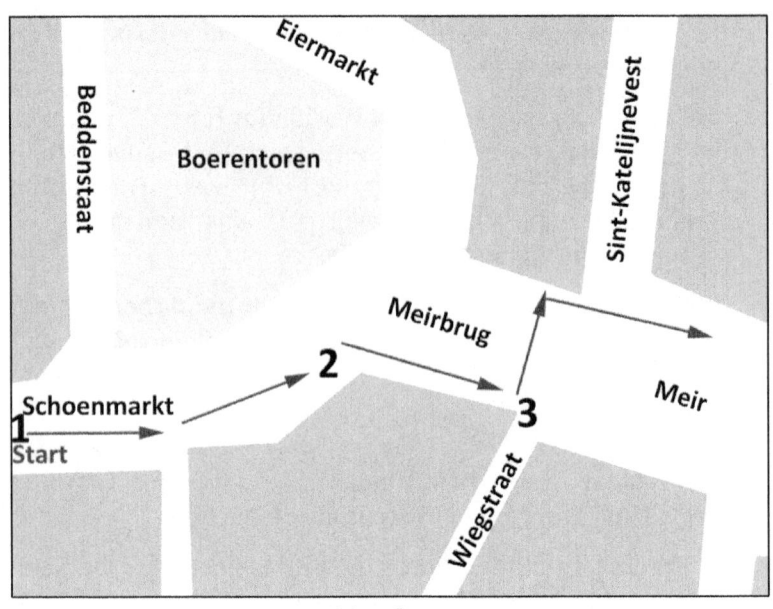

Map 2

Map 2.1 - When you exit the church, turn right to continue along Schoenmarkt passing Schrijnwerkersstraat on your right.

At the next corner you will be directly across the road from the entrance to the Boerentoren which just saw from Groenplaats.

Boerentoren

When the tower was first built it had a panorama room right at the top, and sightseers were charged 3 francs to visit.

The whole tower was restored in the seventies but the new panorama room is not open to the public which is a shame.

At first glance you just see a huge grey tower but look a bit closer to see the art deco embellishments.

The most obvious are almost at ground level where eight gowned ladies seem to be holding the tower up. Further up you can see a frieze running across the tower with plants, flowers, sheaves of corn, and animals.

Mary and the Cross

Now take a look just above the frieze on the seventh floor to find the largest statue of Mary and Jesus in Antwerp. Behind Mary stands a huge cross.

The architects wanted to both continue Antwerp's love of the Madonna sitting on street corners, and to commemorate the beautiful and monumental Cross on the Meir which stood nearby until the late eighteenth century.

Map 2.2 - The Boerentoren bends round following Eiermarkt. But you should stay on the busy main road. It leads away from the tower and you will walk into little Meirbrug which is just one block long.

Where you are standing was originally outside the city boundary and was a swampy area of land called Meir.

People started to build homes here as Antwerp expanded. In the fifteenth century they paved part of the swampy land over, leaving just a canal running down the middle with the Meirbrug crossing over it. Sadly no trace of the bridge remains other than its name.

Map 2.3 - The next street on your right is Wiegstraat. When you reach it use the nearby zebra crossing to cross Meir. Once over, turn right to pass Sint-Katelijnevest on your left.

Meir

This is now Antwerp's main shopping thoroughfare; you might have seen a painting of it on walk 1 if you visited the Rockoxhuis which showed what it used to look like long ago.

The well-to-do built their palatial homes along the street's edges. As time moved on the sewer/canal was covered over and Meir became even more popular with the moneyed classes as it was far more hygienic. Even the Royal Palace was built on this street.

By 1982 however Meir was clogged with traffic and the city fathers made the bold decision to pedestrianize it. Meir held its ground commercially and it's still the place to shop – even if no one actually lives there anymore.

If you do not want to shop or even look at the many luxury stores which you will see on both sides of Meir, there are plenty of beautiful buildings to find.

Just remember to look up past the shop windows to see the decorations, sculptures, and golden statues.

Map 3

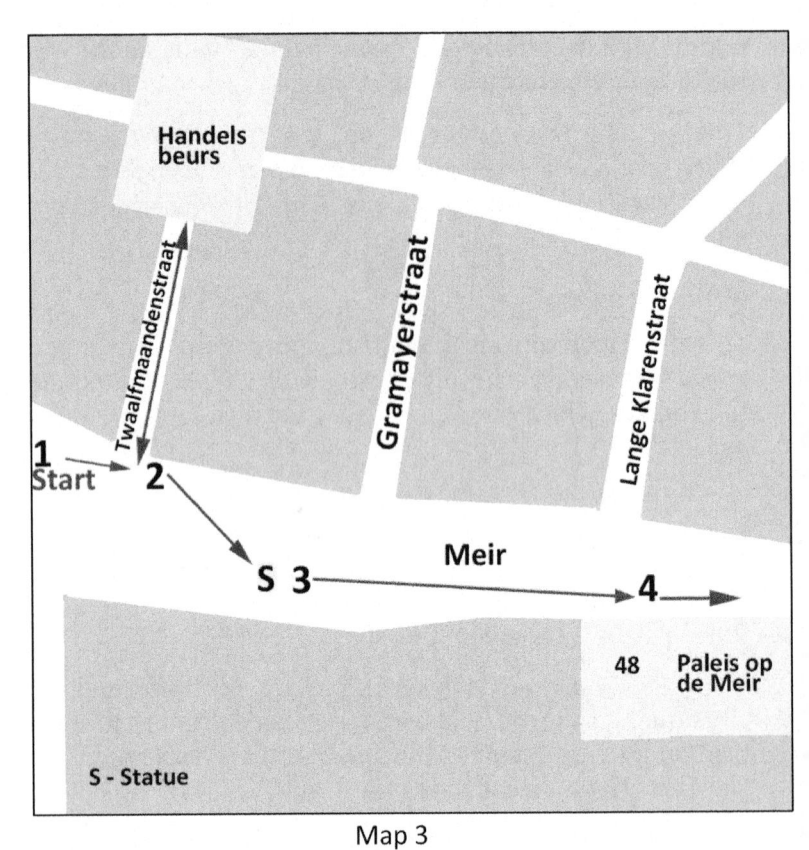

Map 3.1 - The next street on your left is Twaalfmaandenstraat. If you look down it you will see The New Stock Exchange, the Handelsbeurs.

Handelsbeurs

The new Stock Exchange building was the world's first purpose built stock exchange. It was a much grander affair than its predecessor which you might already have visited on walk 1. The new building was completely covered to keep the traders warm and dry. Inside it has a spectacular central hall which is really worth seeing. The hall is huge and it boasts 38 pillars as decoration.

The designers of the London Stock Exchange used the Handelbeurse as its inspiration. It was even called "the bourse" until it was renamed The Royal Stock Exchange by Royal Decree of Queen Elizabeth I.

Unfortunately the Antwerp stock exchange closed and was replaced by the one in Brussels. So this building was left to decay and for a very long time Antwerp mulled over how to make use of it as it was just too beautiful to destroy. At the time of writing the doors are almost open again. It has been restored and you should be able to visit and enjoy its fantastic central hall.

If you want to visit it, walk down Twaalfmaandenstraat and take a look inside. Return along Twaalfmaandenstraat to Meir and turn left when you have had enough.

Map 3.2 – Continue down Meir and not too far along on the right-hand side at number 24, you can see the giant's hand chopped off by Brabo.

The Hand

It makes a good snap.

Map 3.3 - Continue along Meir to number 48 on your right-hand side; it sits opposite Lange Klarenstraat. At the time of writing it is a bank.

Banque de Reports

Originally an artist's mansion stood here, but it was knocked down in 1906 to construct this very ornate building for a private bank. You need to stand back to see its columns, balconies and statues.

The bank was owned by Edouard Thys, an enterprising gentleman who ran about eighty companies all over the world, was a Judge, and to finish things off was also the chairman of Antwerp Zoo. The architect of this building also designed the Zoo, so he was clearly a favourite of Thys.

When Thys passed away, the building was taken over by the Banque d'Anvers which wanted to transfer its headquarters to the prestigious Meir. You can see the intertwined initials "BA" of the new bank incorporated into the wrought-iron just above the doorway. Above that are two carved ladies surrounded by flowers and garlands.

Map 3.4 - Just next door at number 50 you will see the Paleis op de Meir

Paleis op de Meir (The Palace on the Meir)

This gorgeous Rococo building was built for a successful merchant in the eighteenth century. Over the years the building passed from one aristocratic family to another, and each proud owner added their own enhancements.

When the French arrived Napoleon decided this would be his residence, although he never actually lived there. However the improvements he made to the palace just in case he did stay, appealed to the incoming Dutch king. He then added his own embellishments.

A tour is available and if you go on it, you will see that the rooms on the ground floor still have the original Rococo design. The most interesting room is the Hall of the 17 Provinces. The ceiling proudly displays the coats of arms of the provinces which had just been merged to form The Netherlands

Once Belgium gained its independence from The Netherlands, the royal family often hosted grand receptions there. So the building got a new addition, the Hall of Mirrors, which is the most decorative room in the palace.

Even if you don't do the tour, pop in to see the central courtyard which is free – it was enhanced many times by the various owners and is now mainly used by cafes and restaurants.

The palace also now houses The Chocolate Line – fantastic chocs! From the shop you can see into the kitchen where the chocolates are produced. Napoleon loved chocolate, so it's ironic that this palace which he had renovated and intended to live in is now making and selling chocolates.

F - Fountain
V - Vertelboom
W - Wall

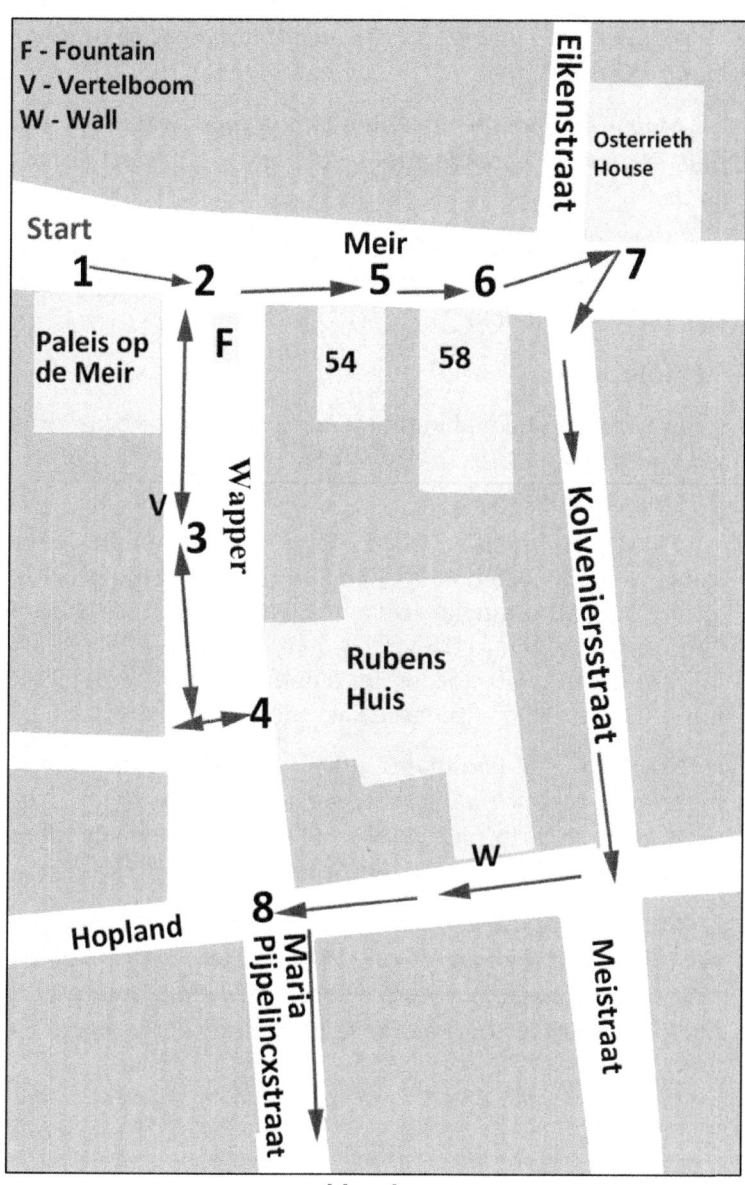

Osterrieth House

Start
1 → 2 → Meir → 5 → 6 → 7

Eikenstraat

Paleis op de Meir

F

54   58

V

Wapper

3

Kolveniersstraat

4

Rubens Huis

W

Hopland   8 ←

Maria Pijpelincxstraat

Meistraat

Map 4

Map 4.1 - When you exit the palace turn right to continue along Meir.

Map 4.2 - Take the next right into Wapper where you will find the lovely Vissende Arend fountain - it means Fishing Eagle.

Walk down the right hand side of the fountain and alongside a white wall. On it you will see a painting which is called the Vertelboom.

Vertelboom

Antwerp is unusual in that it has a City Poet whose job it is to write about life in Antwerp. Peter Holvoet Hanssen was City Poet in 2012.

A Belgian artist called Roel Jacobs invited ten immigrants to Belgium to join him in telling tales while sitting around a gingko tree. Hanssen took those stories and turned them into the verses of a poem called "The Story Tree and the 10 Branches of Wonder" and it is depicted here. Each branch of the tree has a verse of the poem.

Map 4.3 - If you don't plan to visit the Rubenshuis museum, backtrack along Wapper to return to Meir. Turn right along Meir to find number 54 on your right. Continue the walk from "De Cleynen Sint-Arnold" on page 132.

Otherwise pop into the long single storey glass building in the middle of the road. You need to go there either to buy a ticket or to show your Antwerp Card. Then make your way to the Rubenshuis which is on the left hand side of the street.

The Rubenshuis

Rubens, of course, is famous for his paintings of ladies with more curves than most women would want. His family came from Antwerp although he was in fact born in Germany. His works can be found in major art galleries all over the world. Antwerp is clearly proud of him and has turned his home into a lovely museum holding many of his less well known works.

Rubens visited Italy and loved what he saw there. He commissioned this house on his return and made sure it was built in the Italian style. However it was remodelled between Ruben's day and the present day by its interim owners, so Antwerp has made great efforts to restore it to its original style.

As you pass under the archway into the grounds look up to see two statues, Mercury and Minerva, the god of painting and the goddess of wisdom.

When you enter you will be ushered to the start point of a one-way tour round the house and given a good little guidebook of the paintings on view.

You will visit the studio where his students and assistants worked with Rubens to produce over two thousand pieces of art, all with that important Rubens tag. Rubens was always involved in some part of each production. He used his team to paint the simpler parts of the paintings but would execute the delicate important details by himself. If someone commissioned a work only by Rubens, they would have to pay an enormous fee.

Here are some highlights to hunt for.

Collection of Cornelis van der Geest - Willem van Haecht

Haecht was well known for his rendition of private and public art collections. Cornelis van der Geest was a wealthy spice merchant from Antwerp and friend of Rubens. He commissioned Haecht to paint his private collection.

In this painting you can see him proudly showing off one of his paintings to his guests, including not only Rubens but also Van Dyck. The painting being admired is by none other than Quentin Matsys – remember the blacksmith artist from walk one?

We can only assume that Geest's collection wasn't actually all stashed higgledy piggledy in one room as shown here!

Self Portrait – Rubens

You can also see one of the rare self-portraits by Rubens. He was more modest than Rembrandt who did over forty that we know of, whereas Rubens did only four. You can compare it to the depiction of Rubens in "The Collection of Cornelis van der Geest", and see how close Haecht got.

Seneca

Rubens brought this bust of Seneca back from Italy. Seneca was a Roman philosopher and writer although he was actually born in Spain. He had a sad end though, as Emperor Nero accused him of treason and he had to commit suicide.

Rubens was a great believer in Senica's philosophy, i.e. to use self-control and wisdom to handle all that life throws at you. Rubens painted Seneca's final moments using the bust as a model, but you will have to visit the Alte Pinakothek museum in Munich to see it.

The Bagpipe Player – Jacob Jordaens

This is just a fun painting with the bagpipe player doing his best to produce some music – you can almost imagine the caterwauling noise coming from his instrument.

Spot the little face on the bagpipes which looks like it is playing the instrument.

Adam and Eve – Rubens

Rubens has painted Adam and Eve in Eden at the moment Eve is about to take that fateful bite of the apple. You can see the snake curled around the Tree of Knowledge just above Eve.

The vegetation around them provides two handy fig leaves for modesty. Both Adam and Eve are less fleshy than is normal for Rubens.

When you exit the house take time to explore the very pretty garden, you can find a bench and sit down to rest your weary feet. Try to imagine the house as it originally was, standing alone without all the surrounding modern buildings – it must have been idyllic.

Map 4.4 - When you exit the museum, turn right to walk back along Wapper and return to Meir. Turn right along Meir and find number 54 on your right.

De Cleynen Sint-Arnold

This very ornate building is where Rubens's grandfather Jan Pijpelinckx lived. When Rubens and his family returned to Antwerp from Germany they stayed here for a time.

The building is decorated with columns, flowers, scrolls, and at the top is a bust of Rubens, celebrating the building's link with the city's most famous artist.

Map 4.5 - Continue to number 58 on your right – another highly decorated building which has four statues guarding the two doors.

Imperial Continental Gas Association

The company was founded in London and supplied gas to light up the cities of Europe. All the decoration on the building is to do with lighting, and the four statues mark key stages in the history of man making light.

The four statues are in chronological order from left to right.

First is a caveman holding up a torch, and beside him stands a Grecian lady holding up an oil lamp. Above the second door is a man with a lantern from the Middle Ages accompanied by a lady with gas lighting.

Map 4.6 - Continue in the same direction and cross over the junction with Eikenstraat and Kolveniersstraat staying on Meir. Immediately on your left you will find number 85, the Osterrieth House.

Osterrieth House

The house was built in the 16th century and has always been owned by rich merchants or bankers. It's had Flemish owners, Spanish owners, and even Italian merchants have at some time owned and embellished it.

By the nineteenth century, Osterrieth House was the centre of the social life of the rich and the famous. The owner of the house at that time was Madame Osterrieth. She was a patron of the Belgian Antarctic Expedition which

Roald Amundsen took part in. The expedition failed as their boat, the Belgica, became trapped in the pack-ice for a year, and the crew suffered dreadfully and almost starved to death. However they survived and made it back home. Amundsen went on to be first to reach the South Pole on a later voyage.

If you get a map out and have a look at the Antarctic you will see the Osterrieth range, named after Madame Osterrieth.

The house was hit and badly damaged in World War II, and had to wait until 1948 to be rescued by a bank. The bank used the house as offices but it maintained its original features and added to the beautiful interior with two sketches by Rubens. At the time of writing you can visit but only on a Sunday with a guide – ask at the tourist office if you are interested.

Map 4.7 - Backtrack a few steps on Meir and turn left along Kolveniersstraat. You will reach Hopland where you turn right.

Hopland

You will notice the fashion shops such as Armani on all sides. You are now in Antwerp's fashion district and you will see many of the major houses represented. The brick wall you pass on your right is actually the wall of the Rubenshuis garden which you might have visited earlier.

Map 4.8 - Take the next left into Maria Pijpelincxstraat which was named after Rubens' mother.

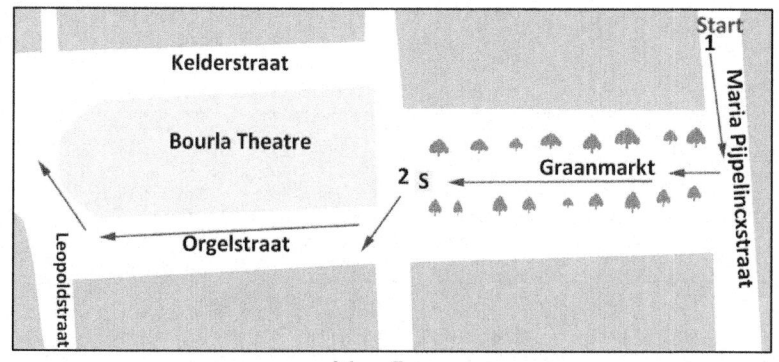

Map 5

Map 5.1 - Take the first right into peaceful Graanmarkt with its double line of trees.

Graanmarkt

This square was a fruit and vegetable market as far back as the sixteenth century and it's another nice spot for a bit of lunch or a drink. If you are here on a Sunday you will find the Vogelenmarkt in full swing. Vogelenmarkt means bird market but these days all sorts of items are for sale.

Victor Driessens

The statue in the middle of the square is Victor Driessens. He was a French actor who worked in Antwerp and later kick-started theatre in the Dutch language – unheard of until then as it was always performed in French. He was appointed director of the National Theatre and remained director for eight years. He then resigned and returned to acting. Sadly he had a stroke on stage and died three days later. His funeral was attended by huge crowds.

Map 5.2 - At the far end of the Graanmarkt is the back of the Bourla Theatre. Walk down the left hand side of the theatre to reach the front.

Bourla Theatre

This area was the centre of Antwerp's tapestry industry from the sixteenth century and the original building which stood here was called the Tapissierspand. It was where the very precious tapestries were stored and traded, not just from Antwerp but from most of the Low Countries.

During the Spanish Fury the Spanish looted it and stole a fortune in expensive tapestries. This was followed by the collapse of trade because of the Scheldt being blockaded by the Dutch.

The tapestry industry never recovered and eventually the original warehouses were given to a charity. It decided to stage theatre productions in it to raise money for Antwerp's poor. However it was small scale.

Once Antwerp had recovered economically a bigger and better theatre was wanted. So the Tapissierspand building was demolished and this new theatre was built on the same site.

At the top you can see Apollo the god of music, and he is accompanied by his nine muses, Calliope, Polymnia, Erato, Terpsichore, Euterpe, Thalia, Urania, Clio, and Melpomene. Below them are busts of the "Heroes of literary and musical drama". Some of those you will recognise are Mozart, Moliere, Schiller, Euripides, Sophocles and of course Shakespeare.

Inside, the theatre is adorned with crystal chandeliers and lots of statuary. The ceiling is especially ornate, painted in bright colours.

It was listed as a protected monument in 1938. However it slipped into decline in the fifties and worse, a new theatre opened opposite it in the eighties. Once again demolition was suggested as the solution; however it was given a reprieve and restored for Antwerp's Year of Culture.

Today the theatre once again has its own company, the Toneelhuis – the name you can see along the front of the building.

Map 6

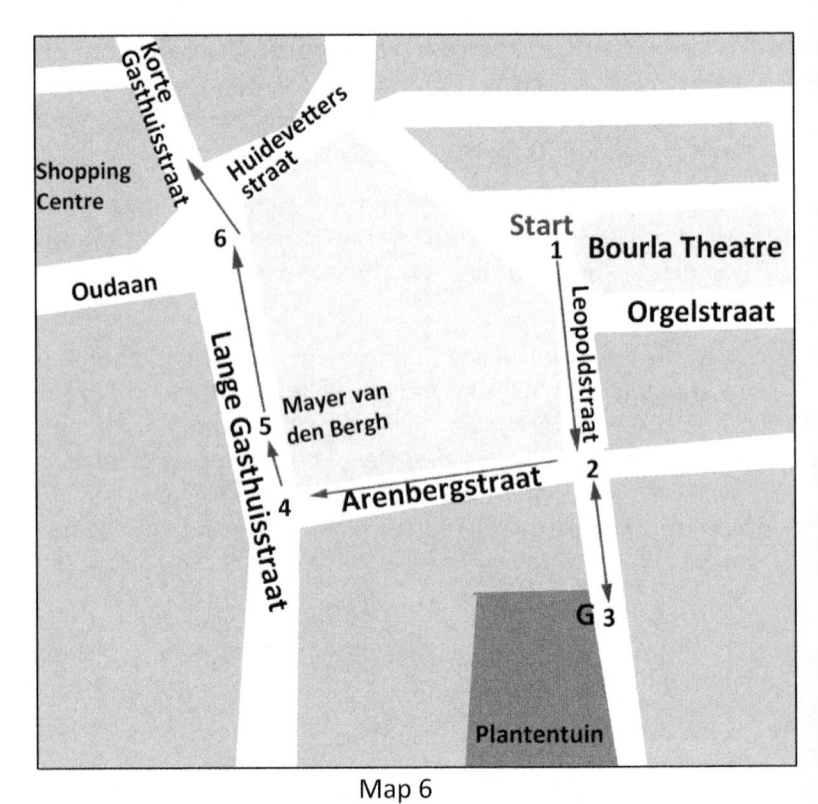

Map 6.1 - With your back to the theatre door, turn left to walk into Leopoldstraat.

Map 6.2 - Cross the junction with Arenbergstraat and just ahead on the right you will see some trees. When you reach them you will find the gate into the Plantentuin.

Plantentuin

This is the Plantentuin, a botanical garden which was built in 1825. It originally had an important role in growing herbs and plants for use in the nearby hospital. Nowadays it still harbours 2000 plants and some are very rare.

There are green lawns, beds full of colourful flowers, cactus filled greenhouses, and a pond which according to legend was used to breed leeches, again for medicinal purposes. Take a wander round and perhaps have a seat for a moment or two in a rare splash of green.

Map 6.3 - Leave by the gate you entered and turn left to backtrack along Leopoldstraat to the junction with Arenbergstraat. Turn left into Arenbergstraat

Map 6.4 - Take the next right into Lange Gasthuisstraat.

On your right at number 19 is the entrance to the Museum Mayer van den Bergh.

If you don't want to indulge in any more art, continue from "Korte Gasathuisstraat" on page 144.

Museum Mayer van den Bergh

This building used to be a private mansion, but is now a museum and worth a visit to see its paintings by Bruegel. However there are also other highlights.

Dulle Griet - Bruegel the Elder

This is probably the most famous piece in the collection although no-one is really sure what it's about, other than everyone is having a gruesome time. Dulle Griet means Mad Meg, and she is in the centre striding across the painting in her armour. Dulle Griet is a Flemish term for a shrew or wild woman.

If you remember the Proverbs painting you saw in the Roxkoxhuis on walk 1, you know that Bruegel was very fond of proverbs. One Flemish proverb is "To tie a devil to a pillow" which meant coping with a man. If you look carefully you will see women tying men to cushions in the painting, while Mad Meg strides forward carrying plates and pans. So perhaps this painting represents the life of Flemish women dealing with their men and their daily tasks – but who knows!

Mayer van den Bergh picked Dulle Griet up for pennies in a Cologne market and then identified who the artist was. Of course it is worth a fortune now.

Twelve Proverbs - Bruegel the Elder

Here is another example of Bruegel's love of proverbs. It's actually a series of oak panels and each panel symbolises a Flemish proverb.

At the bottom right is a man who is "Pissing at the Moon" which means wasting your time in futile activity.

Cornelis de Vos

One of the larger rooms is mainly a set of family portraits by Cornelis de Vos who was one of Antwerp's leading portrait artists – especially of children.

The paintings are beautifully lit and are much more appealing than family portraits are generally.

Joris Vekemans was a wealthy business man from Antwerp and this is his family. The costumes the children are wearing are so elaborate with ruffs and lace and the two boys have hats.

The boys are wearing dresses which seems odd to us but was normal practice in those days – for practical reasons! It was quite a family ceremony when a boy pulled on his first pair of trousers, usually about the age of seven.

Herodias Revenge – Juan de Flandres

A very Flemish looking Salome presents the head of John the Baptist on a plate to her stepfather Herod and her mother Herodias.

Herodias gets ready to cut the tongue out. She hated John the Baptist because he had called her a sinner for marrying her brother in law.

Herodias had asked her daughter to grant Herod's wish and dance for him, in return for the death and head of John the Baptist. Salome obligingly performed her infamous dance and was given the head as payment. Oddly, Herod seems shocked when presented with the result.

Shrove Tuesday - Hieronymus Bosch

This is an exuberant painting of carnival – the riotous time of making merry before the frugality of Lent kicks in. It's a European tradition which still goes on to this day.

Just look at all those scowling and grinning faces, and the dancing couple in the middle are fascinating.

Korte Gasthuisstraat

Map 6.5 - With the museum door behind you, turn right along Korte Gasthuisstraat and walk to the next junction.

Map 6.6 - Here you will see tramlines heading off to your right-hand side, and slightly to the left stands a very modern shopping centre made of cube shapes.

Keep the shopping centre on your left and walk into a pedestrianised section of Korte Gasthuisstraat.

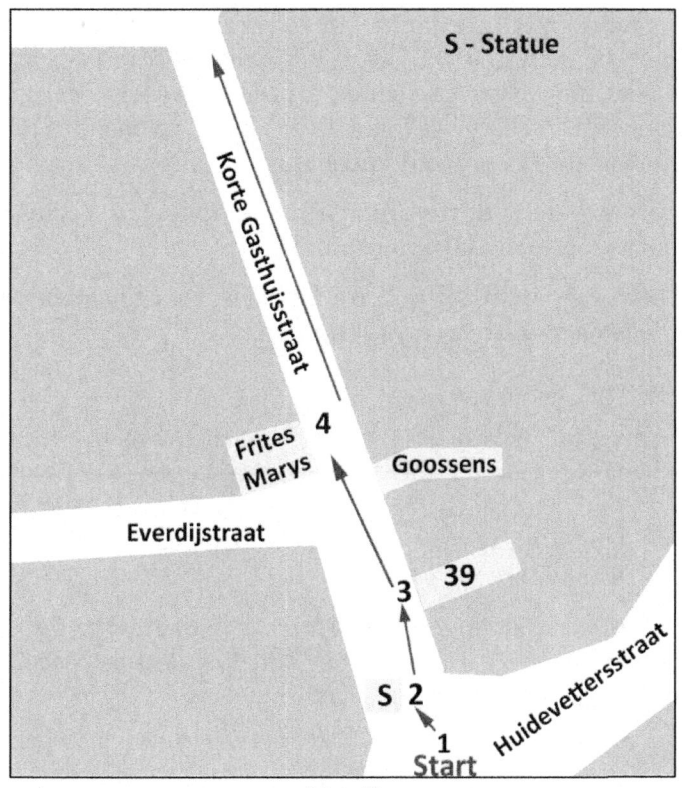

Map 7

Map 7.1 - As you enter Korte Gasthuisstraat you will be greeted by Den Deugniet – he is standing on a plinth just outside the shopping centre.

Den Deugniet (The Rascal)

It's a cheeky little statue of a young boy dropping his trousers to show off his backside. It's relatively new as it only appeared in the seventies but was an immediate success. It's said to bring luck if you rub the statue's backside, but that may be just a joke on tourists by the locals.

145

A folk singer called John Lundstrom wrote a song about Den Deugniet in 1976. The words stand next to the statue but are only in Dutch and don't translate very well. Perhaps because of The Rascal's fame he has been stolen more than once, but so far has always been recovered.

It's now perhaps time for a little self-indulgence and this area provides several opportunities.

Map 7.2 - Walk along Korte Gasthuisstraat to number 39 to find Philips Biscuits on your right.

Philips biscuits

This little bakery is a great favourite with the locals, perhaps because of the ever changing window display made out of biscuits. If you fancy something sweet you could try an Antwerpse Handje - remember the legend of Brabo's hand?

Map 7.3 - Continue along Korte Gasthuisstraat. On the corner of the next street on your left, Everdijstraat, you will find Mary's Chocolate Shop.

Mary's

Mary Delluc started her chocolate shop in Brussels in 1919. Her chocolates were so good she was awarded a Royal Warrant by King Leopold II, one of the few chocolatiers to have that honour.

There are now branches in all of Belgium's major cities - there are even a couple in Japan. The Antwerp branch opened in this very old gabled house which is named The White Angel and which dates from 1621 – it's dated by the plaque above the first floor windows. If you haven't indulged in chocs yet, this is another good option.

Opposite Mary's is Goossens Bakery.

Goossens bakery

This is one of the most popular bakeries in town. It's also the oldest as it started in 1884 and is still run by the same family. You may have to queue a while but it's worth the wait. Everyone loves the raisin bread or the suikerbrood (sugar bread).

Next door to Mary's is Frites Atelier.

Frites Atelier

If you prefer savoury to sweet then this frites shop is a favourite. It's quite new but a big hit with the locals.

Map 7.4 - Continue along to the end of Korte Gasthuisstraat to reach another crossroads.

Map 8

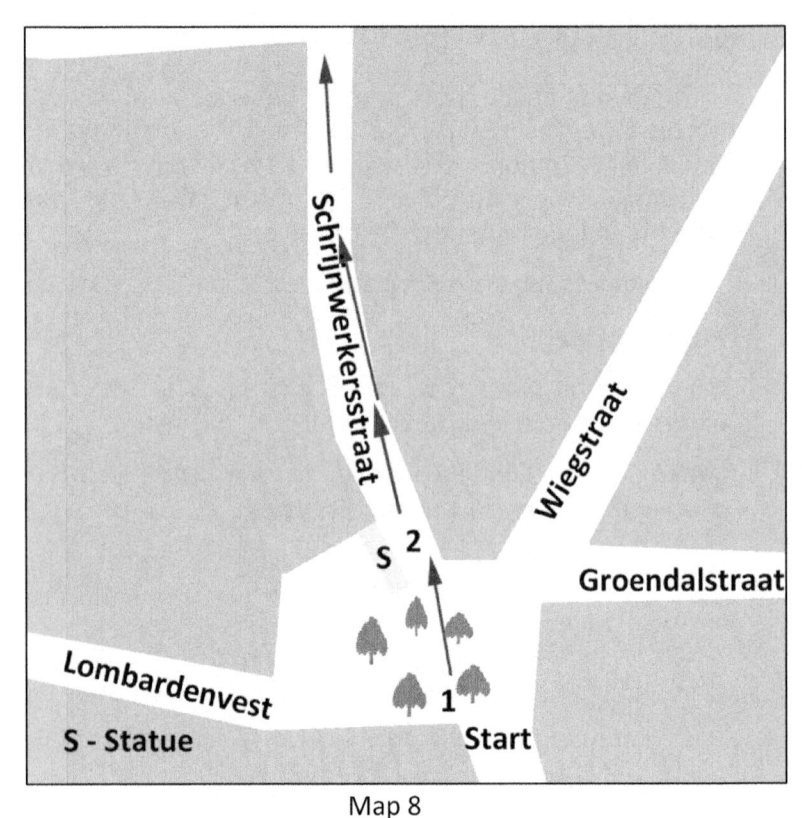

Map 8.1 - Walk through the trees and straight ahead towards Schrijnwerkersstraat.

Schrijnwerkersstraat

The street name means Carpenter's Street as this street is where the Carpenters Guild House stood until 1612 when they moved to Hoogstraat. You might already have seen that guild-house if you have already done Walk 2.

At the start of this street you will find a wall on the left-hand side; and on it a depiction of the crucifixion. It was put there in 1710 but most of it has been replaced piece by piece over the centuries.

Map 8.2 - Continue to reach the end of Schrijnwerkersstraat.

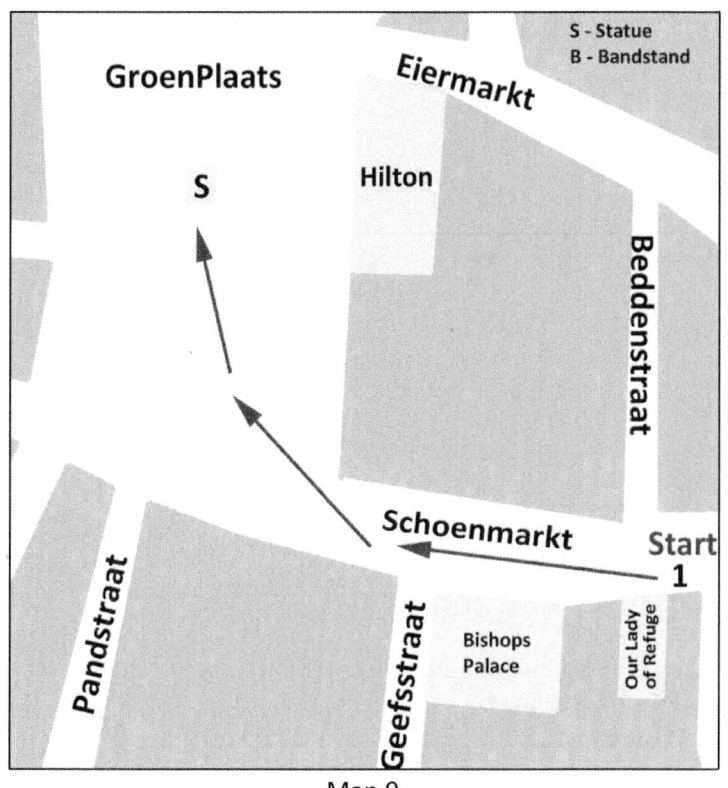

Map 9

Map 9.1 - At the end of Schrijnwerkersstraat turn left into Schoenmarkt and walk along to Groenplaats where this walk ends.

Walk 5 – Eclectic Architecture (1km)

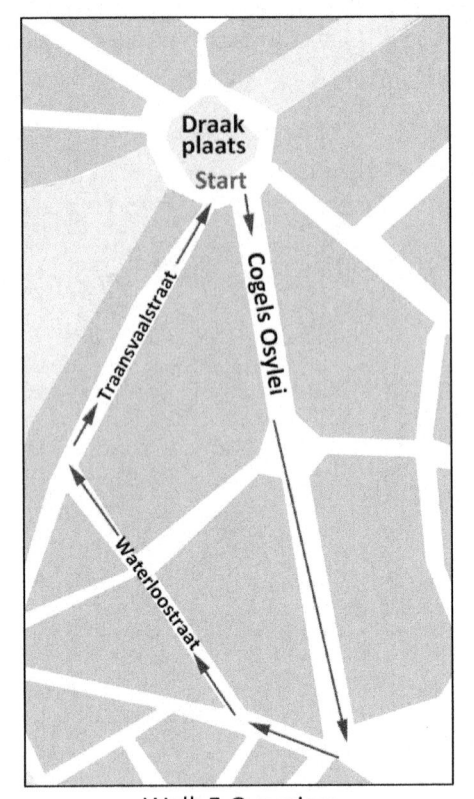

Walk 5 Overview

When you have had enough art, history, and just want a gentle stroll somewhere pretty, pick a pleasant sunny day and travel to Antwerpen Draakplaats by tram.

This walk will guide you around Antwerp's very individualistic mansions which were mostly built at the end of the nineteenth century. The whole area was designated a protected urban site in the eighties.

At the time of writing you can catch tram 6 or 11 to get to Draakplaats. However please check the latest timetables and routes.

Map 1

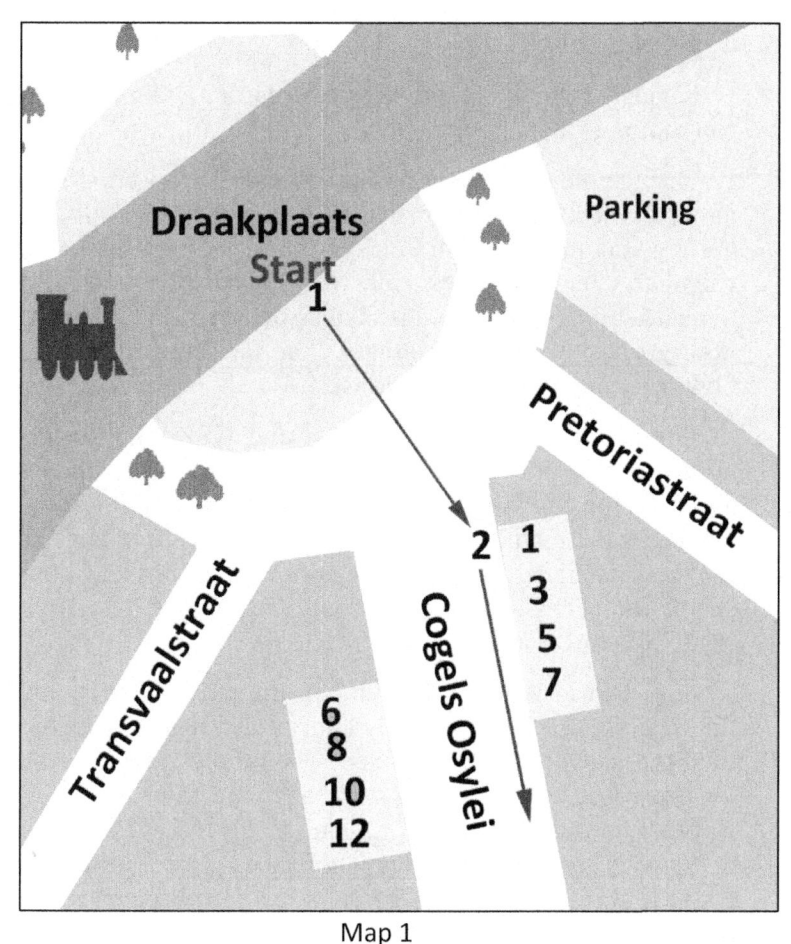

Map 1.1 - When you exit the tram you will be under a railway bridge.

Follow the tram lines in the same direction that your tram is heading for, and you will walk into a street named Cogels Osylei.

Cogels Osylei

Cogels Osylei is named after two banking families who were joined via marriage.

They owned the land here and planned an ambitious new commercial development. However it turned out that no-one was interested in investing in it. So instead it was used to build homes for the very rich by the "Société Anonyme pour la Construction de Maisons Bourgeoises", which translates as "Limited Company for the Construction of Bourgeoise Houses".

The result is that Cogels Osylei and two other streets which form a triangle are packed with expensive houses and mansions in different styles of architecture. Most of the mansions were built in the late nineteenth century, and the architects seemed to have indulged in their own and their clients' fantasies – hasn't everyone dreamed of living in a castle or a tower at some time!

After World War II this area became quite derelict, and the result was a plan to simply knock the houses down and turn the area into office blocks. Thankfully this caused a huge protest from Antwerp's citizens, and the savvy ones stepped in and snapped up the empty houses which were being sold very cheaply. The whole area gained protected status and the houses have been restored and renovated to their former glory. As you explore you will see that whereas the houses are all very individual, they mostly have the same little garden gates and railings.

Here are some of the best to pick out.

Map 1.2 – Walk down the left-hand side of Cogels Osylei.

Number 1 - Brabo House

On your left is Brabo House and above the door stands a bronze statue of Brabo tossing that giant's hand again. He seems to be almost welcoming you to explore Cogels Osylei.

Numbers 3, 5, 7

Next door you will see a set of three houses made of a light brick which are jazzed up with red and black bricks which really brings the façade to life. The middle one is called Den Ooievaar, as it states above its door.

Numbers 6, 8, 10, 12 - Carolus Magnus

On the other side of the street is another set of houses but this time they have been built as a symmetrical group.

Above the two middle doors are some mosaics which proclaim the name "Carolus Magnus" and above them is a statue of their namesake Charlemagne

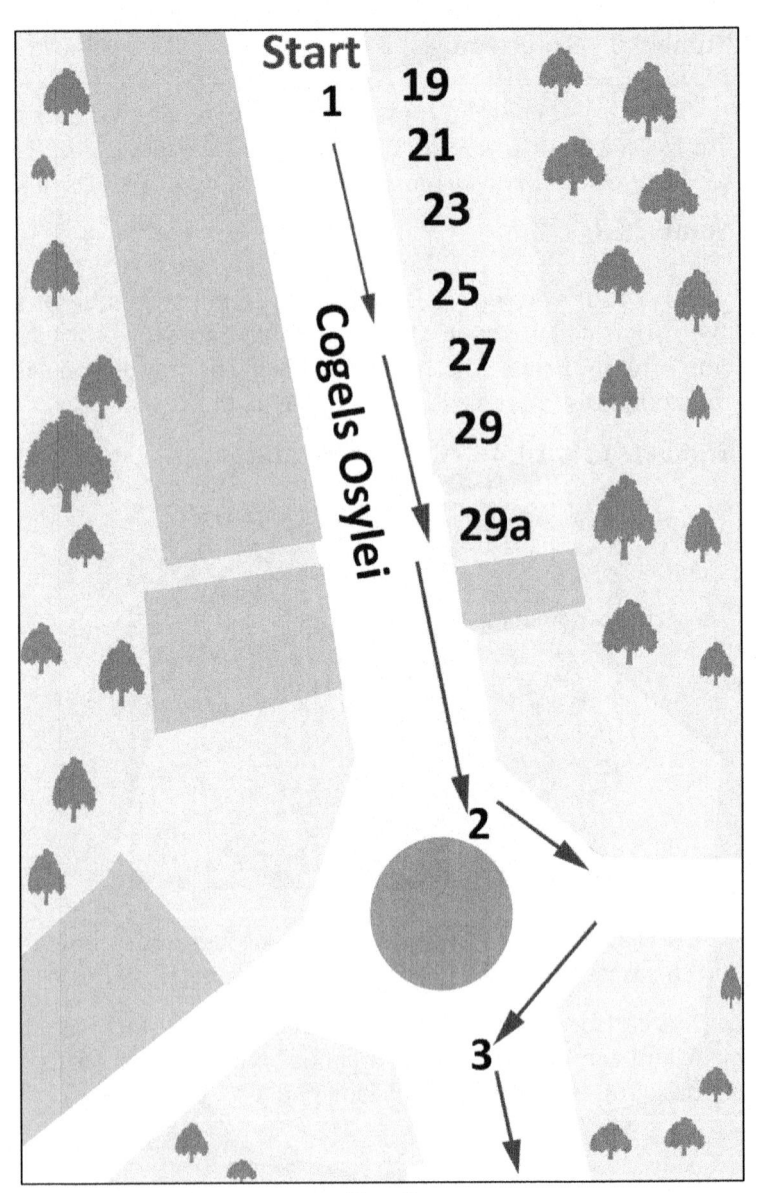

Map 2

Map 2.1 – Switch your gaze back to the left-hand side of the street to find Number 19-23.

Here are four houses which were built as one unit and made to look like an Italian palazzo. The god Apollo is strumming his lyre centre-stage.

Numbers 25, 27, 29

Next along is another ensemble of three houses, this time looking like a castle from Sleeping Beauty. The three houses are called "In de Sterre", "de Sonne", and "de Mane".

Number 29a

This house is very different from those you have seen already. It was built after World War II and before the area was protected, meaning the architect and builder could indulge themselves, and they did. This house is much more modern than anything around it and splits opinion; you either love it or hate it.

Map 2.2 - You will reach a roundabout with four matching buildings on the crossroad corners.

Map 2.3 - Cross the roundabout to continue along Cogels Osylei.

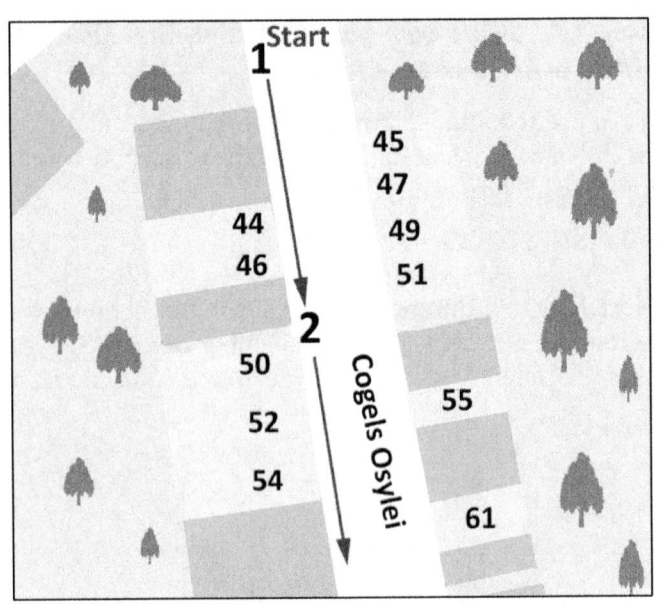

Map 3

Map 3.1- Pass a building on your right which is quite hidden behind trees and shrubs – perhaps to stop tourists staring at it.

The next house to find is number 44 which sits just next to it.

N

Number 44 – Iris de Lischbloem

Look up to see the very unusual gable which is an isosceles triangle which is topped with an Iris. The facade is decorated with fish, shells, and flowers. The house name is above the door.

Number 46 – De Roos

Just next door is the Rose. It has a wonderful wavy iron balcony which has a canopy, above which you can see some iron roses. Underneath the canopy are more roses on the stonework. It also has curving stonework around the door.

It was built for Belgian Edouard Myin who competed in the shooting events in the 1900 Paris Olympics, but unfortunately didn't win any medals.

Numbers 45, 47, 49, 51 - Boudewijn with the Iron Arm

Opposite De Roos and Iris stands a huge construction which is actually four different houses, but built to present a castle like appearance.

Baudouin with the Iron Arm was the first Earl of Flanders and his statue stands in the middle. He eloped with Judith, the daughter of King Charles the Bold. The king was not amused, as he expected his daughter to marry someone much more important. He had them both excommunicated, so the lovers in desperation travelled to Rome to plead their case with the Pope.

The Pope listened with a sympathetic ear and reversed the excommunication. Just as importantly, he wrote to Charles the Bold asking him to accept the couple. They finally got the King's consent to marry, although the King could not bring himself to attend the happy ceremony.

Map 3.2 - Next up on your right are three houses which celebrate nature.

Number 50 - De Zonnebloem (The Sunflower)

This Art Nouveau house is decorated with golden sunflowers and is beautiful – the sunflower plant above the door is particularly beautiful. The house helpfully has its name above the first floor window.

Number 52 - De Tulp (The Tulip)

This house was owned by Eugène Joors who specialised in still life paintings of flowers, so he popped an iron tulip on top of his home.

Number 54 – Het Klaverblad (The Cloverleaf)

This house has lovely stained glass windows. Look up to the first floor to see the expected cloverleaf. Beneath it states "This House is Called Clover Leaf".

Opposite, the nature theme continues with De Morgenster

Number 55 – De Morgenster (The Morning Star)

This small house stands out from its neighbours because of its Art Nouveau style. Right at the top are the very unusual circular windows – almost like portholes on a ship.

Above the first floor windows is a tiled panel which did at one time have an image of a morning star which is a small yellow flower. However that image has been replaced by plain tiles – what a shame.

Number 61 – De Zodriem (The Zodiac)

This lovely house is topped with an iron globe surrounded by the signs of the zodiac.

Map 4

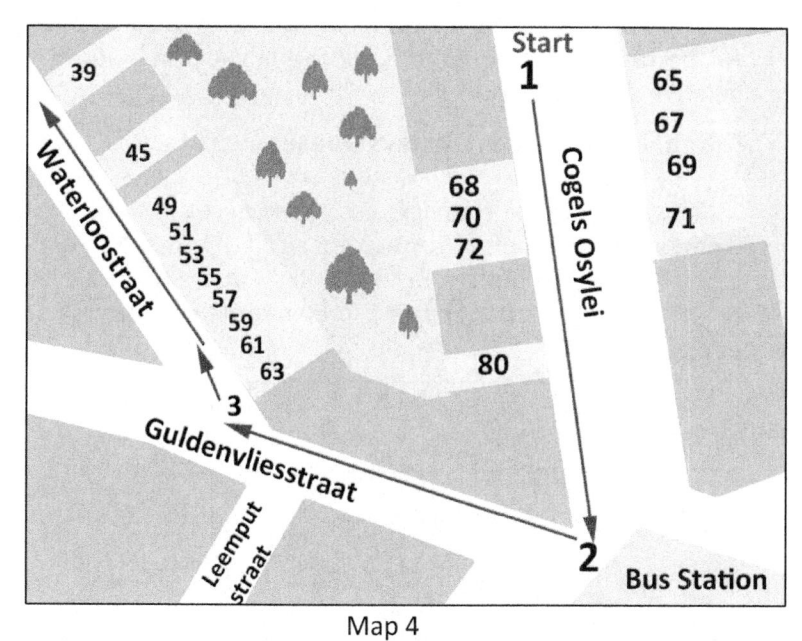

Map 4.1 – Continue along Cogels Osylei and look to your left.

Number 65,67,69,71 – Scaldis

This is another multi-house construction. It's called Scaldis which was the name given to the Scheldt River by the Romans. Up at the top are sculptures of mythical figures including Poseidon.

Number 68 - Sint-Jozef

Opposite stands a red brick and white stone house called Sint Jozef. The bay window on the first floor holds a statue of the saint.

Number 70-72 - De Biekens

Next door stand two mirrored houses which have a gorgeous art nouveau sculpture striding across both doors. At the top is a white panel with the house name above a beehive and buzzing bees.

Number 80 – Quinten Matsys House

This is a very Art Nouveau house which really stands out from its neighbours. It was inspired by Art Nouveau buildings already built in Brussels. Right at the top is a bust of the Flemish artist who is commemorated in the house name.

As you read on Walk 1, Matsys had to prove to his prospective father-in-law how good an artist he was. He proved his ability by painting a portrait of his father-in-law to be, and added a fly to the painting. When shown the painting, his future father-in-law thought the fly was real and tried to shoo it away! To celebrate his skill, the ironwork balcony below his bust has a fly worked into design.

Map 4.2 - When you reach the end of Cogels Osylei you will see a bus station in front of you. Turn right along Guldenvliesstraat following the tram lines.

Map 4.3 - Take the first right into Waterloostraat.

Waterloostraat

This street was created in 1897 and it was named after the famous defeat of Napoleon. The houses are not as grandiose as Cogels Osylei but there are still interesting oddities to see.

Number 63, 61, 59, 57, 55 - Den Tijd (The Weather)

Right at the start on the right-hand side is another ensemble of five houses. They are individually called The Morning, The Day, The Time, The Night, and The Evening. Look up to see the house names on the colourful tiled panels.

Number 53

This is a little Art Nouveau house with typically decorative window and balcony.

Number 51, 49 – Baeckelmans

Both these houses were designed by Joseph Baeckelmans for his mother. Look up to see the blue tiled panels which decorate both houses.

The architect was executed by the Germans in 1915 as a spy working for the resistance. He was executed at the National Shooting Range which the Germans used in both world wars to despatch captured spies. The British nurse Edith Cavell was also executed there.

Number 45

This house catches your eye from some way away because of its green and yellow glazed bay window and iron balcony which make the house seem quite exotic.

Number 39 - Les Mouettes (The Seagulls)

Here is another wonderful balcony set in the wall which undulates outwards to accommodate it.

The house is decorated with a mosaic of a water scene with a rising sun, seagulls and rocks. The name of the house appears above the balcony.

Map 5

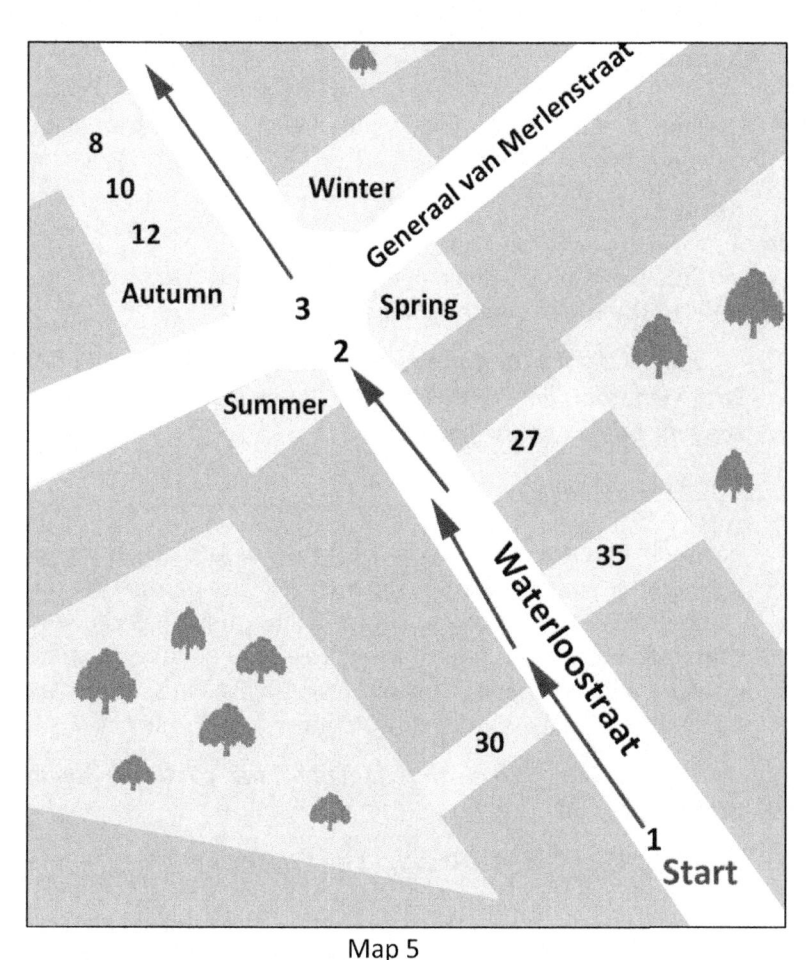

Map 5.1 - Continue to reach number 30 on your left-hand side.

Number 30 – Napoleon

On the other side of the street you can see a mosaic of Napoleon himself on the top floor. He stands behind two cannons.

Number 35

This one is quite simple but has a dinky little stone balcony.

Number 27

This has a much more ornate façade and balcony. Look right to the top to see the panel of storks.

Map 5.2 - A little further on you will reach a crossroads with Generaal van Merlenstraat. Pause to look at each of the four houses on the junction.

The Four Seasons

Each house is decorated with one of the seasons and each states which season it represents. The paintwork and stained glass windows of spring and summer are green, and those of autumn and winter are brown. They have seasonal flowers and a mosaic representing the season. They all have fantastic bay windows protruding into the street.

Map 5.3 - Cross the junction to continue along Waterloostraat.

Number 12, 10, 8 - De Pauw (The Peacock)

The first house at number 12 has another splendid wooden bay window on the top floor. Number 10 has one on the first floor, and number 8 has to make do with a balcony but also has a tiled image of a peacock which is where the building gets its name.

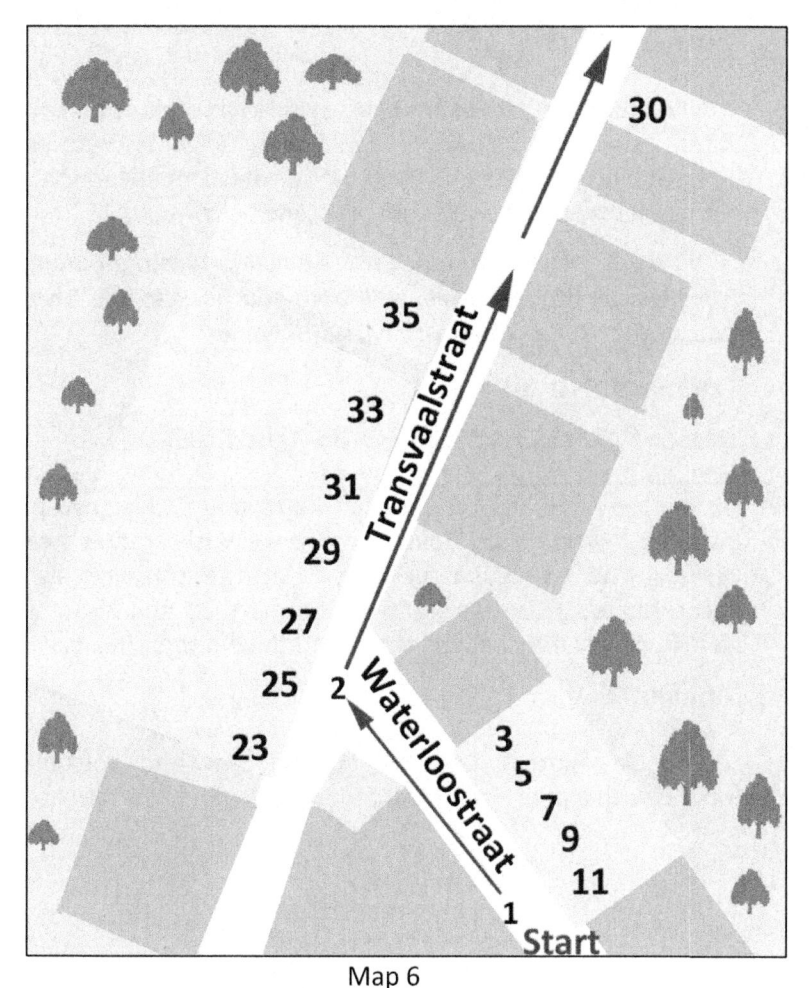

Map 6
Map 6.1 - Continue along Waterloostraat.

Number 11 - House of the Battle of Waterloo

This house represents the battle the street is named from. Above the bay window is a very colourful mosaic, showing us Napoleon facing Wellington as well as the name of the house.

Number 9,7,5,3

This building has lovely patterned brickwork. The two outer houses on this building have fantastic gables with an integral balcony. The two inner houses have smaller gables but make up for that with a lovely stone balcony.

Map 6.2 - When you reach the T-junction turn right along Transvaalstraat. This street will take you back to the tram stop, but is itself packed with beautiful homes

Traansvaalstraat

Number 23, 25, 27, 29, 31, 33, 35 - The Greeks

The long building on your left-hand side is designed in the style of a Grecian temple complete with statues and vases. The triangular pediments at the top are also decorated with Grecian figures. Numbers 23 and 35 even have two caryatids balancing the building on their heads.

Number 30

Here is another fantastic bay window and balcony, topped with a mosaic of a woman watching the sun set.

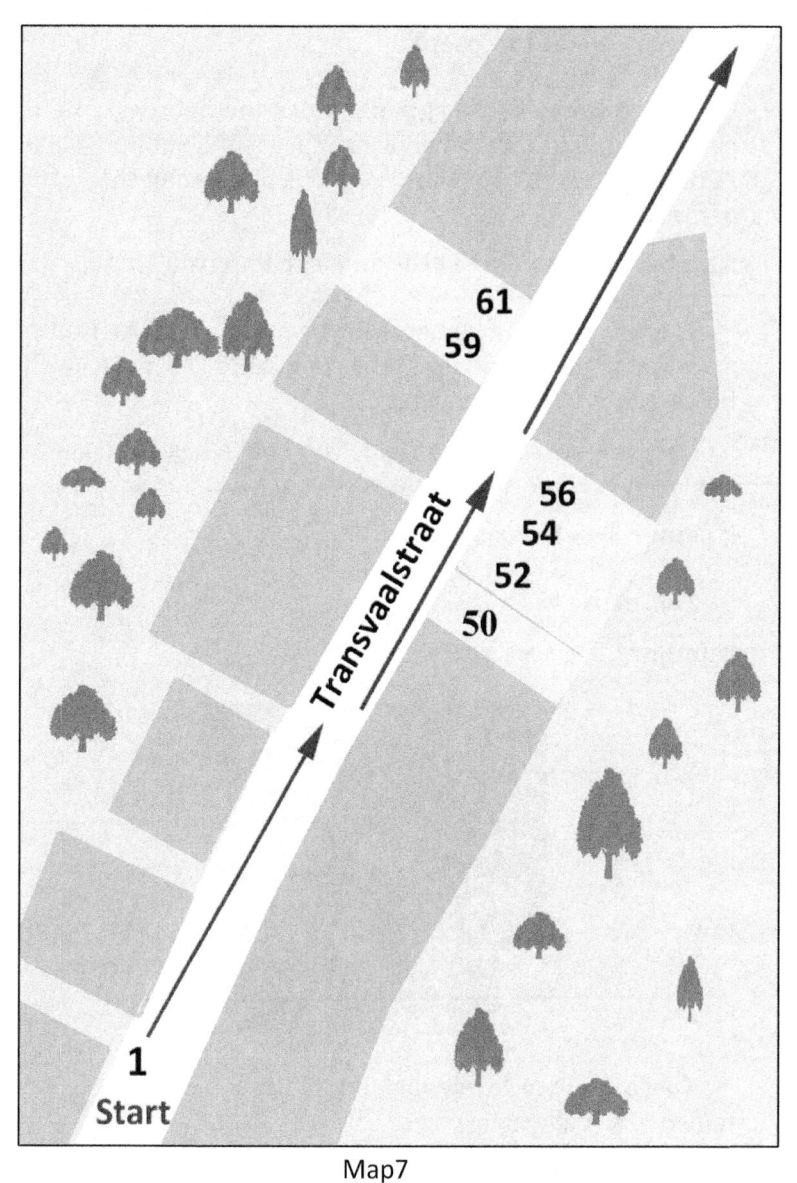

Map7
Map 7.1 - Continue along Transvaalstraat to reach number 52 on your right.

Number 50 – Saint Joseph

This house has Saint Joseph above the doorway. He of course was married to the Virgin Mary and on either side of him you can see a lily – his symbol representing the purity of his wife.

Number 52, 54 – The Lotus and The Papyrus

This is a pair of homes with beautiful window frames and tiled panels. Look up to the roofline to see more lovely flowers interspersed along it.

Only the house on the right, The Lotus, has its name on the façade in blue and yellow tiles.

Number 56 – Boreas House

This house has a striking narrow bay window.

Number 59, 61 – The Twelve Devils

These are two lovely matching houses. Look up to see under the balconies where twelve devils are grimacing down at you.

Map 8

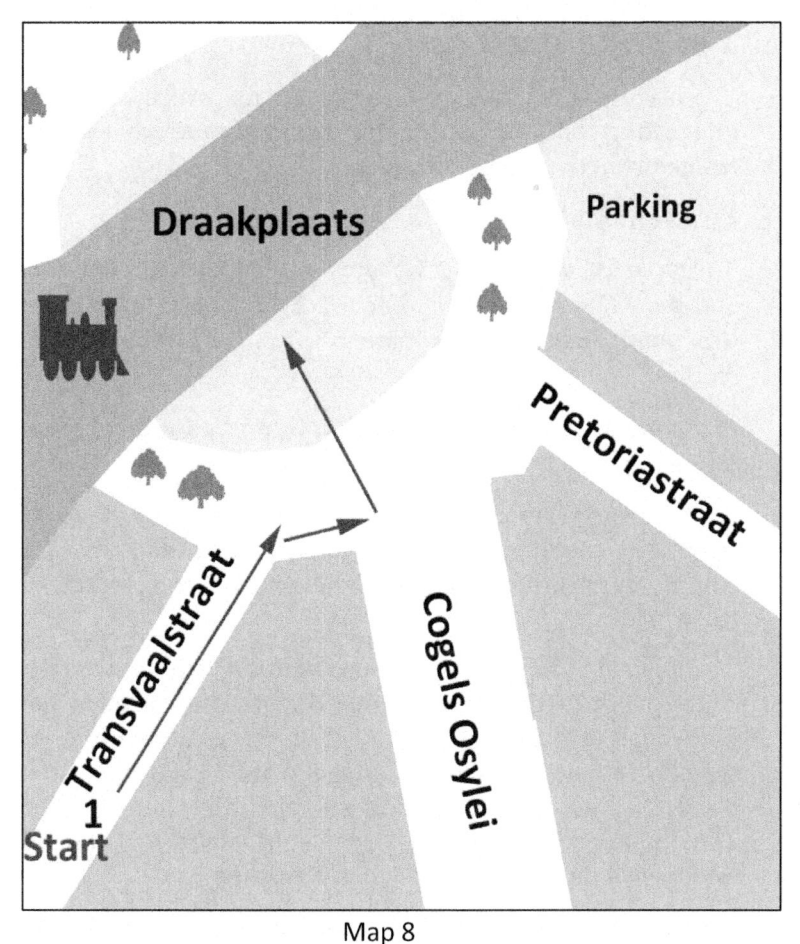

Map 8.1 - Keep walking along Traansvaalstraat and you will return to Draakplaats.

Here you can find some cafes if refreshments are needed, and of course the tram-stop where you can catch a tram back into town.

Too far to Stroll to

Antwerp has some individual sights which are very interesting but you need to venture onto the public transport network to get to them.

Centraal Station

You may actually be staying in a hotel near Centraal Station. If not, you can reach it by taking a tram from Groenplats to Koningin Astridplein which lies just outside the station.

At the time of writing, trams 3, 9, and 15 will take you there.

The train station exemplifies station design in the early twentieth century – built with style and grandeur. It's commonly regarded as one of the most beautiful stations in the world.

Originally, in 1836, Antwerp station was a wooden construction with just 4 tracks. Now it is nicknamed the Cathedral of Stations and is constructed with different types and colours of stone and marble. Even along the tracks the decoration continues with little stone turrets. The station now has three levels of platforms and an impressive moving pavement between them.

It's worth noting that this grandeur is all a result of a recent restoration. Like most of the world the automobile swept train travel aside in the last century, and the station was scheduled for demolition. However, it was saved in 1975 and became a listed building by royal decree. The ambitious restoration project started in the eighties.

The enormous dome was made of copper but that was taken by the Germans in WWII. Its slate replacement wasn't really rainproof and the interior suffered as a result, so during the renovation it was restored to its pristine state with red copper.

The station's original marble floor was lifted and stored away during the renovation. Sadly not enough care was taken, and a lot of the marble was stored in freezing conditions which it didn't survive. The original stones which made it are now in the centre of the floor, and the rest of the stones are new - after a long and extensive search to find marble which matched the originals.

If you would like to see the station used for more than just travelling, have a look at this link - You need headphones.

http://www.youtube.com/watch?v=0UE3CNu_rtY

KMSKA

KMSKA is the Royal Museum of Fine Arts Antwerp and is a treasure house of art. Even though Old Antwerp is full of wonderful art, you might find it irresistible to venture to the south of the city to visit this museum. At the time of writing, tram 4 will take you there.

You can easily spend a few hours here browsing around the masterpieces. Here are some favourites to track down:

Madonna surrounded by Seraphim and Cherubim – Jean Fouquet

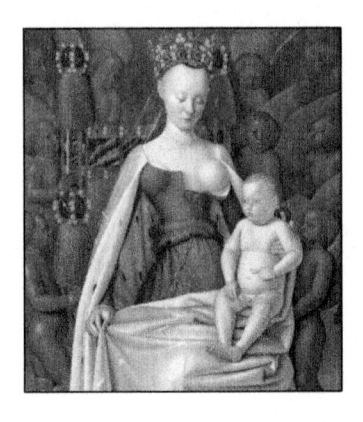

This is one of the most famous paintings in the collection.

It was painted in the fifteenth century and was actually part of a diptych, a two panelled alter piece. The other half is now in Berlin but is not nearly as interesting as this half - it shows Etienne Chevalier who commissioned the diptych and his patron saint.

It's thought that Agnes Sorel, who was thought to be "the most beautiful woman in the world", and who was the mistress of Charles VII of France was the inspiration for the Madonna. She had actually died two years before the painting was created.

The Madonna is very fashionably and richly dressed with a jewel-encrusted crown and an ermine cloak. Her hair is shaved away from her face which might seem odd to us now, but was a highly fashionable hairstyle in the fifteenth century. A high forehead was seen as incredibly beautiful so fashionable ladies shaved their hair back to heighten the forehead.

The ornate throne she is sitting on and the angels surrounding her are in blue and red, in sharp contrast the unnatural whiteness of skin of Mary and Jesus.

The Fall of the Rebellious Angels – Fran Floris

This was part of a triptych which once hung in the Cathedral. It was badly damaged during the fury of 1566 and only this panel survived. It shows a scene from the Revelation of Saint John when the archangel Michael leads other angels to fight the Rebellious angels with a dragon thrown in for good measure. Archangel Michael is centre-stage at the top.

Take some time to look at the details of the painting as they are intricate and fascinating. From the many heads of the dragon wrapped around Michael's legs, to the writhing snakes and animal heads of the Rebellious Angels.

Peasant Woman digging Potatoes – Van Gogh

Before Van Gogh travelled to Southern France where he painted most of his best known works, he tried painting the impoverished people around him in Holland. He produced several works of the peasants trying to survive on their poor diet of potatoes, and the back-breaking work it took to get them.

Intrigue – James Ensor

If modern art is more to your taste you will probably like this one. It looks like a wedding scene with the happy couple in the middle surrounded by friends. It is an unsettling picture because the figures are all wearing masks, which is always a creepy vision. It's similar to the uncomfortable feeling some people get when faced with a grinning clown. Ensor was very fond of putting masks on his figures, perhaps because his mother ran a little shop which sold them.

Christ with singing and music-making Angels - Hans Memling

This triptych has Christ in the middle with six singing angels and they are flanked by ten other angels playing all sorts of instruments; lute, harp, fiddle, trumpets and others. The four angels with puffed-out cheeks who are blowing into various flute-like instruments look like they are really going to blast out a tune.

Did you enjoy these walks?

I do hope you found these walks both fun and interesting, and I would love feedback. If you have any comments, either good or bad, please review this book.

Other Strolling Around Books to try:

- Strolling Around Amsterdam
- Strolling Around Arles
- Strolling Around Antwerp
- Strolling Around Bath
- Strolling Around Berlin
- Strolling Around Bilbao
- Strolling Around Bruges
- Strolling Around Delft
- Strolling Around Florence
- Strolling Around Ghent
- Strolling Around Jerez
- Strolling Around Lisbon
- Strolling Around Ljubljana
- Strolling Around Lucca
- Strolling Around Madrid
- Strolling Around Palma
- Strolling Around Pisa
- Strolling Around Porto
- Strolling Around Sienna
- Strolling Around Toledo
- Strolling Around The Hague
- Strolling Around Verona